William L. G. Smith

Observations on China and the Chinese

William L. G. Smith

Observations on China and the Chinese

ISBN/EAN: 9783337166977

Printed in Europe, USA, Canada, Australia, Japan

Cover: Foto ©Suzi / pixelio.de

More available books at **www.hansebooks.com**

OBSERVATIONS

ON

CHINA AND THE CHINESE.

BY

W. L. G. SMITH,

LATE U. S. CONSUL AT SHANGHAI.

NEW YORK:
CARLETON, *PUBLISHER*, 413 *BROADWAY*.
(LATE RUDD & CARLETON.)
M DCCC LXIII.

Entered according to Act of Congress, in the year 1863, by
GEO. W. CARLETON.
In the Clerk's Office of the District Court of the Southern District of New York.

TO

HON. LEWIS CASS.

I dedicate this volume to you, in token of my respect for your private virtues, and gratitude for your friendship.

W. L. G. SMITH.

CONTENTS.

CHAPTER I.

PRELIMINARY. 18

CHAPTER II.

THE TREATY OF WANGHIA. 20

CHAPTER III.

THE POSITION OF THE UNITED STATES IN OPENING THE COMMERCE OF CHINA. 25

CHAPTER IV.

FOREIGN TRADE OF CANTON. 30

CHAPTER V.

THE GENERAL FEATURES OF CHINA. 81

CONTENTS.

CHAPTER VI.

THE YANGTZE KIANG. 85

CHAPTER VII.

THE SHEPHERDS OF CHINA. 88

CHAPTER VIII.

LAND TITLE.— CURRENCY.— THE EMPEROR'S GENEROSITY. 40

CHAPTER IX.

THE AVOCATIONS OF THE CHINESE. 47

CHAPTER X.

THE EMPIRE.— THE EMPERORS.— KIND OF GOVERNMENT.— IMPERIAL ABODE.— THE EXECUTIVE OFFICERS —THEIR REGALIA AND DUTIES.— THE ARCHIVES. 53

CHAPTER XI.

QUALIFICATIONS OF THE MANDARINS.— THE COURT LANGUAGE. OFFICIAL DELINQUENCY.— ADMINISTRATION OF JUSTICE. . 62

CHAPTER XII.

THE JUNK CASE.— CIVIL SIDE OF COURT. . . . 70

CHAPTER XIII.

THE WIDOW WOMAN.— CRIMINAL SIDE OF COURT. . . 74

CHAPTER XIV.

RAILROADS.— COURIERS.— FORMALITIES.— THE YAMUNS. . 79

CHAPTER XV.

CHINESE PECULIARITIES.— POLYGAMY. 84

CHAPTER XVI.

HOW THE CHINESE GET THEIR WIVES.— THE MARRIAGE CEREMONY.— THE MARRIAGE FEAST. 87

CHAPTER XVII.

HOLIDAYS.— HOW TIME IS RECKONED. 91

CHAPTER XVIII.

AMUSEMENTS.— TEA HOUSES.— OPIUM.— DINNER PARTIES. 93

CHAPTER XIX.

THE VARIOUS TRADES.— ROADS.— HOUSES.— CATTLE.— MODE OF DOING BUSINESS.— COOLIES. 97

CONTENTS.

CHAPTER XX.

THE REBELS.— TAEPING WANG. 103

CHAPTER XXI.

THE NEW TREATIES. 110

CHAPTER XXII.

HOW THE NEW TREATIES WERE RATIFIED.—TAKU FORTS. 113

CHAPTER XXIII.

SHANGHAI. 122

CHAPTER XXIV.

SQUEEZES. 131

CHAPTER XXV.

CANTON. 136

CHAPTER XXVI.

HONG KONG. 143

CONTENTS.

CHAPTER XXVII.

FOO-CHOO-FOO.— TEAS.— THE DIFFERENT KINDS. . . 147

CHAPTER XXVIII

AMOY. 151

CHAPTER XXIX.

NINGPO. 153

CHAPTER XXX.

SWATOW AND TAIWAN.—TYPHOONS.— FORMOSA. . . 155

CHAPTER XXXI.

CHIN KIANG.— KIN KIANG.— HANKOW. . . . 161

CHAPTER XXXII.

TANGCHOW.— CHEE-FOO.— TIENTSIN.— THE EMPEROR.— NEW-CHWANG. 166

CHAPTER XXXIII.

THE COAST.— PIRATES.— CHUSAN . . . 180

CHAPTER XXXIV.

PUNISHMENT.— YEH.— HO. 187

CHAPTER XXXV.

RELIGION. 197

CHAPTER XXXVI.

BOTANY.— MINERALOGY. 204

CHAPTER XXXVII.

THE FUTURE. 209

CHINA AND THE CHINESE.

CHAPTER I.

PRELIMINARY.

JOURNEYING from one's own country into foreign lands was formerly a grave affair. The traveler set out upon his pilgrimage with many a solemn preparation, and bade farewell to all as if never to return. Such has been the improvement in the construction of vessels and in the art of navigation since the commencement of the present century, that now the traveler leaves home with almost as little preparation or ceremony as if taking a drive to some neighboring town. He pays his passage money, takes his ticket, and steps aboard of the ship that is to carry him over thousands of miles of water, with the same vivacity that he would go to a fair, picnic, or fashionable Spa. Neither the storm-clouds over a soundless sea, nor an angry ocean, create terror.

What may have been heard or read of dismasted, foundering, or capsized ships, is dismissed from the mind and crushed away as a mere phantasy of the imagination. The increased speed of travel shortens the former duration of the voyage; and the traveler now goes bounding over the same seas which in former times cost so many weary and lingering days to the argonaut. With the barometer to forewarn the calm and the gale, the sunshine and the storm — the chronometer to point the time, and the compass to guide the helm — the mariner unerringly keeps the vessel on its course. If bound to the other side of the globe, he doubles the Cape of Good Hope, once the great stumbling-block of the navigator, as easily as Cape Ann: and the voyager finds himself gliding along the coasts of Java and Sumatra, and flying with a favorable monsoon up the China Seas, before he has hardly finished the last publication issued from the press on the eve of his departure from his native land. He is now farther than the farthest limits of Alexander's conquests. He is beyond the far off Indus, and is on the confines of that country spoken of in the sacred records of the Old Testament as the land of Tsin or Sinim. He is among a people strange and new to him, though their national existence dates back at least sixty centuries.

It was in the month of May 1858, that the writer of this embarked at New York on board of the American clipper ship " Mandarin " bound to China. One hundred days, it was thought, was the shortest time for the duration of the voyage. But this good " clipper " was tight, staunch and strong: had her hatches well caulked and covered, her sails new, an experienced master and a trusty mate, faithful under officers and a nimble crew, and well furnished with all things needful and necessary for the voyage. On the ninety-second day from New York, the ship cast anchor in the harbor of Hong Kong, having sailed nearly eighteen thousand miles. We were landed on a hemisphere where everything is in movement, where fortunes are made and spent, where the extremes of wealth and poverty meet, where the arrangement of society, is radically the reverse of what exists in these United States of America. It does not take a very long time to comprehend that one is among strange and distinct races, born and bred under different religious and political institutions, amenable to different laws, and indulging different usages. The dissimilarity is so great in all the leading features of national polity and society, that it is hard to institute a comparison. It is only in things which run parallel to those in his own country, that a comparison can be instituted; and charity too often fails where criticism begins.

China has many characteristics totally unlike any other country. With a long line of record, she carries us far back on the track of time, as we attempt to become acquainted with the prominent events of her history. Although the Jesuists have wandered up and down her valleys and plains, and over her hills and mountains for two centuries, mingling with the population, becoming familiar with their customs and manners, their laws and institutions, and with the people themselves, yet, after all, the Ta Sing empire, of China as it is usually called, has remained a sealed book to "outside barbarians." The Portuguese were the first of the Western nations to reach it. They were the pioneers to India, and having reaped a rich harvest there, they ventured to the Islands of Java and Sumatra, and picking their way over becalmed waters and hidden rocks and shoals, they finally emerged, through the straits of Gasper, Banca and Malacca, into the China Sea, and reached Macao. They lead in the van of Eastern commerce.

Their object was trade. The native rulers disliked their coming, discouraged intercourse with them, and imposed many restrictions. For several generations the Portuguese and those merchants of other Western nations who followed in their wake, trafficked with the people of China under many serious disadvantages. They could deal only with such of the Celestials as were authorized by the government to trade with the "barbarians." The celestial authorities encouraged the idea that the western merchants were worse than "barbarians," they called them "devils." Every impediment was interposed against the foreigner in the conduct of his business. He was watched in all his movements and transactions, subjected to arbitrary and heavy imposts, not allowed to reside within the walls of the seaport town, nor suffered to go among the people at large. If he was misused, his complaint was laughed at. If he was robbed, either ashore or afloat, no effort was apparently made to recover the stolen property or to punish the offender. His traffic was continually hampered by unjust edicts. The exchange of commodoties was made with a few *hongs*, and they were constantly informed that they must refrain from visiting other ports under pain of confiscation of property and loss of their lives. When admitted into the presence of a Mandarin, however low his position, they were invariably required to *kotow* and *chin chin*, or no notice was taken of them or their complaints. Regarded more as pilgrims to Mecca with tribute and incense to gain the favor of these lords of the east, they were regarded as menials, and not unfrequently treated with contempt by all classes.

But, the Western mind, then as now, was not inactive. It scanned the future, and trade of magnificent proportions loomed up, enough to gratify the most extravagant imagination. Experience taught the enterprising merchant that ships could traverse the Southern Atlantic and the vast Indian Ocean with the same certainty of speed and safety as they could sail upon the Mediterranean, and other inland seas. It was evident that a country of dense population had been reached, and that the products of the West would find a ready market. In return, there was an abundance of silk of excellent quality, and, as it seemed, an almost measureless quantity of tea. There were also precious stones and pearls, and mechanism of the most exquisite workmanship. Experience demonstrated the important fact that the Chinese were fond of trade, and quite ready to barter off their teas and silks for the productions of the Western hemisphere; and what was of far greater importance, it was found that there was a wide and pleasing margin between the cost and selling prices. There was a large net profit on the cargo carried thither, and, at first, a fabulous profit in the rich cargo brought hither in return. In addition, it was found that there was at all times a ready market at the termination of both outward and homeward voyages. The obstacles, therefore, interposed by the cool and subtle mandarin — the restrictions imposed upon traffic, the exclusion of the foreign factor and supercargo from entering the Chinese exchange — all had a contrary effect from what was intended, and, instead of dampening the energies or cooling the ardor, were fresh stimulants to move these courageous and enlightened adventurers of Europe and America, and impelled them to make, and to renew from time to time, their herculean efforts, at least to share, if not to monopolize this dazzling commerce of the extreme East.

CHAPTER. II.

THE TREATY OF WANGHIA.

GUIDED by a Providence whose secrets are locked up in the deep abyss of eternity, and actuated by that quenchless love for humanity which has flowed along the ceaseless current of time through every age, from that of Adam until now, the leading powers of the Western hemisphere, namely, Russia, France, Great Britain, and the United States of America, turned their attention eastward, and sought, by diplomacy accompanied with suitable demonstrations of force, to open wide the gates which had so long been closed to the efforts of philanthropy and the commerce of the globe.

These great powers, after much prevarication and the loss of some blood and treasure, succeeded in concluding treaty stipulations with Chinese authorities, that provided for more unrestricted trade, and conferred greater privileges upon their people who might seek those distant shores. Caleb Cushing, a distinguished citizen of the state of Massachusetts, was commissioned by President Tyler in 1843, to go to China and negotiate a treaty of amity and commerce. Furnished with a man of war to support him in his diplomacy, he succeeded in gaining from the celestial authorities a favorable hearing, and in concluding a treaty at Wanghia in the kingdom of China. By the terms thereof, the Emperor conceded to citizens of the United States who should visit or sojourn in that country, the right of exterritoriality. Under this concession, the citizen at all times is under the laws of his own country. He is not amenable to the laws or institutions of paganism, nor subject to the summons, order, or dictation of its officials. Whatever may be his short comings, or however at fault he may be in fulfilling his obligations, whether to the Chinese government, or its subjects, or to any one else, he is still under the direction and order of his own government. Under this treaty, the citizen could visit other ports than Canton, where trade had been confined so long, and therefore was enabled to have the benefit of more markets than one, and to reach in person a wider field for trade. The ports of Amoy, Foo Choo, Ningpo, and Shanghai, were opened to foreigners, and the right to trade at Canton was also recognized by express stipulation.

Provision was also made for the right to hire lands and buildings, and to have Christian churches and burial grounds; and for the accomplishment of those purposes, a proper portion of the land at each of these ports was provided for, and all to be and continue without hinderance or molestation from the Chinese local authorities. Ships and vessels of all classes were allowed to anchor and unload and load at discretion, in whole or in part, without hurt or trouble; and if attacked by pirates on the coast, it was provided that every effort should be made by the Chinese authorities to arrest and punish the guilty, and to recover and restore to the rightful owner, the plundered property. If Chinese become indebted to the citizens of the United States, they were to be made to pay the same, and if they committed depredations either upon the person or property of the citizen, they were to be visited with proper punishment. In return for these concessions by the Emperor, all merchandise was subject, both inward and outward, to an import and export duty, and the ships and vessels to a tonnage duty, and the land to an annual tax — all to be paid into the Imperial exchequer. The ships and vessels were made liable for all the duties, and could not leave port until the same were paid, and the proper port clearance was granted. The land was made liable for the land tax, and in case of non-payment when due, the land reverted to the lord of the soil. Citizens were to be obliged to pay their indebtedness to Chinese, and to be punished for their delinquencies, both civilly and criminally, by their own authorities. In short, the laws of Christian civilization at once were, pro tanto, extended over the realm of paganism, and both were to exist and be executed, side by side, among the children of the sun. What, before then, would have been pronounced by any sane mind a chimera and utterly impossible to be carried out in practice, was now to be set in motion, and the laws of the antipodes of this wide world, were now to be administered in unison on the same spot of earth. The officials of lands thousands of miles apart, educated in entirely opposite schools of morality, laws and politics, and accustomed to totally different schools of thought and reasoning, were now to walk hand in hand, and in truth jointly rule the community.

The population of each nationality, subject only to the jurisdiction of its own flag, was now to form one community and one sociality, and to work, live, and trade in unison, as if under a common allegiance to the same municipality and the same commonwealth.

CHAPTER III.

THE POSITION OF THE UNITED STATES IN OPENING THE COMMERCE OF CHINA.

AFTER the lapse of three centuries, from the time when Vasco de Gama of Portugal first sighted Cape Comorin, the extreme land's end of southern India, and during all of which period every effort had been made, and every danger encountered, both on sea and on land, to gain the good will and enjoy the trade of all the Indies beyond the Cape of Good Hope, at last this rubicon of civilization was reached and crossed. Christopher Columbus planted the flag of Portugal, in advance of all others, upon the shores of America. Turning from the west, the same flag was the first to lead the way over unknown seas into the vast regions of the East. Whilst Portugal and other nations of the Western hemisphere were endeavoring to learn the people and possess the wealth

of the Eastern, young America was being born; and
ere it was out of its swaddling clothes, with a feeble
navy to steady its toddling gait, and a scanty exchequer to defray the expenses of its administration, it
was recognized as a Power among the nations. The
fame of the great infant Republic had reached the
" Flowery Land ; " and it was reserved for her glorious, and, I trust, immortal banner, to be in the van
of this great work of bringing into the family of
nations the oldest of all. She stood at the font in
the majestic cathedral of Christian civilization. Not
content to act as a mere witness to this big event in
the annals of Christendom, undazzled by the glitter
and regalia of royalty, and unawed by the arms and
trappings of war, she quietly and firmly took her
position upon the same dais with Europe and Asia.
To her eternal honor among the good and the just
of all the earth, and to the lasting humiliation of
the British Isles, this prodigy among the governments of mankind was the first to unrol the magna
charta under which the merchant and the priesthood
— as well the native as the foreign — were hence-
forth to dwell together in unity and friendship.
Without the firing of a single shot, or the crossing
of a single bayonet, the stars and stripes, in the calm

but proud consciousness of a giant's strength, waved over the treaty ports of China.

It must not be supposed, however, that this transaction came of itself. The Portuguese, the Spaniards, the Dutch, the English and the French, successively and in turn, had penetrated the country from the Indian Ocean. The Russians had traversed Tartary and Mongolia, and crossed from inland the boundaries of the Celestial Kingdom. The missionary of the Christian religion, with different forms of worship, had wandered into different parts of the Empire, and mingling with the people, became more or less familiar with their language, disposition and customs. From all these sources, the Chinese in return, by their inquisitiveness and aptitude to learn and imitate, acquired much knowledge of the character and resources of Europe and America. Their mechanism, philosophy, and theology were of a different type; and preferred and venerated for antiquity, had been handed down from generation to generation, from a mythological age. It would have been in contravention of the usual laws of humanity and the natural principles that usually govern the actions of mankind, if the Chinese had acted otherwise. But, nevertheless, intercourse with the "outside barbarian " however restricted, tended to weaken if it did not remove, the barrier that separated the races ; and while the merchants of the various countries were carrying on a mutually satisfactory trade, and the disciples of the Christian religion were quietly disseminating the precepts of our Savior, the enlightenment of Christian civilization imperceptibly permeated the mind of stoicism and idolatry, and awakened the attention of the Chinese to the fact that there were other countries and populations, other governments and institutions, not tributary and wholly independent of their own, in other and distant parts of the globe. Hence, the Chinese rulers, and the people, if they had not imbibed more or less desire to improve their relations with the Western hemisphere, at least were apparently willing to do so, and were the better prepared and able to comprehend the necessity of some convention between the several governments regulating the intercourse of the people with each other, and prescribing the relation of one to the other, and the rights and duties of all. The arrangements, both verbal and written, that had theretofore from time to time been made, were very imperfect, and occasioned much dispute and trouble. The opium war with Great Britain was the sequence of ill-digested and patched-up treaty stipulations, full of loop holes, and so designed and left by both parties, and neither party intending to act in good faith further than necessity and present interests might require. Such a line of policy was short-sighted on the part at least of the foreigner, as it tended to lower the foreign standard of right and integrity in the eyes of the Chinese, who,— officials and unofficials — were always on the watch to overreach and cheat in trade, and ready to evade the stipulations upon the smallest pretext.

CHAPTER IV.

FOREIGN TRADE OF CANTON.

CANTON, thus far in all the foreign intercourse of China with Western nations, had been the chief emporium of trade, and the principal centre of evangelical effort. Here were the leading factories of the foreign merchants, and the chief seat of missionary authority. Here were the inlet and outlet of merchandize as it was imported and exported from and to the four quarters of the globe. Here property to the value of over 150,000,000 of dollars annually changed ownership; and here ships were constantly arriving with the productions of Europe and America, and departing heavily laden with rich cargoes of the teas and silks of Asia. But now the circle of legitimate trade was to be enlarged. Other parts were to be essayed, and other fields gleaned, and both merchant and missionary sighed for the anxiously looked-for harvest in the dim distance before them.

CHAPTER V.

THE GENERAL FEATURES OF CHINA.

IN treating of this extensive and important country, it will be useful to take a general survey of its natural qualities and geographical features. These are distinguished by their grandeur and variety. It has regions that bask beneath the brightest rays of a tropical sun, and others that partake of the dreariness of the polar world. The varying degrees of elevation produce here the same changes that arise elsewhere from change of position on the earth's surface. Its plains and dales yield the double harvests and the luxuriant foliage of the torrid zone. Its undulating hills and lofty mountains — often terraced even to the extreme summits — bring forth the fruits and grains of the temperate climates, whilst the lower steppes and heights are covered with the groves of the tea and mulberry. The upper steeps of its mountain ranges are clothed in the south with tallow, sandal, camphor, and other valuable tropical trees and woods, and in the north with the pine and hemlock of the Arctic zone. We do not in China, as in Africa and the polar regions, see nature under one uniform aspect; on the contrary, we have to trace her gradual, yet rapid transitions between the most opposite extremes that can exist on the surface of the same planet. It is, as it were, an epitome of the whole earth. It is more prolific in some parts than in others. This occurs, not so much because of climate or locality, as of use and age. Approaching China from the southward, we are surprised at the barren and uninviting aspect of the country. We behold hills and an undulating surface of land stretching away as far as the eye can discern, without verdure, and sun-burnt — the rocks worn smooth by the elements, the very stones covered with moss — the earth itself blackened and withered and wrinkled with old age. The visitor feels that he is now indeed in an old, a very old country, and this sensation creeps all over him. Everything looks old. The people, no matter of what age, both afloat and ashore, the boats, the san-pans, the junks, the luggers, though now launched upon the waters for the first time, all seem hoary with time, and then, struggling to throw off this nightmare pressing so heavily upon the mind, the eye contracts its vision from a survey of country and water, and lighting upon humanity, catches a rapid glimpse of its covering; and the visitor — fresh from the life-giving and soul-inspiring country on the opposite side of the globe — bewildered with the raiment and costumes of thousands of human beings before him, at once bethinks himself of what he has read and heard of ancient times, and involuntarily begins to fancy that his Charon, instead of ferrying him some eighteen thousands of miles from one hemisphere to another, actually has jumped the wide gulf that divides ancient and modern times, and in a jiffy introduced him into the audience chamber of the Patriarchs of antiquity!

These romantic conceptions, however, soon turn out to be illusory. Upon a closer examination, and rambling away from the coast into the interior, the traveler soon discerns that he is among a live community; and, though clad in habiliments totally unlike those worn to-day in his own country, that even this community is fresh and vigorous, and ready for all the associations of thought and action. He soon learns that he is in one of the most remarkable regions that exist on the surface of the globe. He finds that the varied grandeur of its scenery, with the rich and copious productions of its soil, if equalled, are not surpassed in any other country. He discovers also, that it is extremely probable that it was, if not the first, at least one of the earliest seats of civilization, laws, arts, and of all the improvements of social life. And yet he learns that these have at no period attained to the same pitch of advancement as among the nations of the West, but have, nevertheless, been developed in very original and peculiar forms, displaying human nature under the most striking and singular aspect.

The strong interest which China in itself is thus calculated to excite, must to us Americans be greatly heightened because of its nearness to our shores. Since the acquisition of California, the distance apart, as the bird flies across the Pacific Ocean, does not exceed seven thousand miles.

Of all the Treaty Powers, with the exception of Russia, China and America are the nearest neighbors, and we shall presently see more similarity of thought and action than at first glance would appear probable between a Christian and pagan nation.

CHAPTER VI.

THE YANGTZE KIANG.

THE heart of China — the chief region of her matchless fertility, and once the seat of her Emperors, is composed of the large country watered by the Yangtze Kiang, her great river, and is known as the great plain, all over this extensive empire.

The Yangtze pours through the valley for a distance of over fifteen hundred miles, a continually widening stream, which, during the rainy season, covers a great extent with its fertilizing inundation. From this deep, rich, well-watered soil, the sun, beating with direct and intense rays, calls forth an almost unrivalled power of vegetation, and makes the lower valley yield at least twice a year bountiful crops of rice and cotton, and wheat and beans. Large and populous cities dot the country, and are the marts of commerce and manufactures.

As if to ensure an exuberant fertility to the soil, the Yangtze is not solely dependent upon the rains of autumn and spring for its volume of water, but is annually supplied from the snows of Thibet and Tartary; and when these reach the great valley, the water attains a still greater height, and the river expands into a wide sea, overflowing its banks on either hand for miles.

These never-failing productions supply the immediate wants of a population of over 100,000,000 of souls. Not enough rice, however,— the great staff of Eastern life — is supplied from this source, and the people necessarily look to Siam to furnish the deficit.

Every year, for some time past, from fifty to sixty ships come from the land of the elephant and lion laden with rice, and always find a market in China, and especially in central China. The large outlay for this added to the millions of taels annually expended for the opium of India, would long since have impoverished the country, and in the end reduced it to a state of beggary and famine, among the high as well as the lower classes, were it not for the teas and silks. These commodities always commanding ready buyers and remunerative prices, according to quality, more than balances the account and leaves a surplus for the maintenance of this vast population. As the provinces in the south supply a large export of sugar — in the north of bean cake, which is used for both provender and manure — and all portions of the country of the fruits and vegetables indigenous to their several latitudes, embracing those usually grown in tropical countries, together with innumerable rivers, bays and inlets, abounding prolifically with fish, both scale and shell, of the best quality, and readily obtained, whilst the herds of cattle and sheep on land with the poultry and game, are always forthcoming to fill the larder; all these supplies, the history of centuries shows are sufficient for the wants and necessities of this vast multitude of people now numbering, according to the records of the census at Pekin, full 400,000,000, and comprising one third of all the human race on the face of the whole earth.

CHAPTER VII.

THE SHEPHERDS OF CHINA.

THE mountain scenery of China in general, though wanting the features which invest those of the United States with such awful and sublime character, is nevertheless beautiful, striking and picturesque. Rarely ever rising above the limits of vegetation, its highest summits are crowned with woods and verdure; though over a considerable portion there is distributed rock, forest, and jungle, still the greater part is under cultivation. The pick-axe, the iron rake and the hoe, are in constant requisition, and more used in breaking up the soil and meliorating it for the seed and the plant, than the plow and the harrow. The ground whether sown or planted, is usually raised into beds like those usually seen in American gardens, and is daily manured from the time the bed is finished till the produce, whatever it may be, has attained maturity. The use of not a single foot of land is overlooked, nor its tillage omitted. Everything, animal and vegetable, that is not used in some other way, is turned to the account of manure, and sprinkled over the earth.

There are no fences usually, not even the hedges so common in Europe. The cattle and sheep are stalled most of the time. Occasionally they are led out to clip the isolated tufts of grass, or glean some wheat or bean field lately harvested, or browse upon the cotton shrub after the last picking. They are watched lest they may go into forbidden ground, and in due time are returned to the stable. The children are the shepherds of China.

CHAPTER VIII.

LAND TITLE. — CURRENCY. — THE EMPEROR'S GENEROSITY.

ALL the land in the Empire belongs to the emperor. It is leased to the occupant. The title deed is a perpetual lease, subject to forfeiture in case the annual rent of 1500 cash per mow is not paid. This cash is a copper coin of the size of the old American cent, except that it is thinner, and is coined at the Imperial mint, and is the usual currency for the settlement of small balances arising from work or trade, among the generality of the people. A square hole is made through the centre, and are thus conveniently strung together; and when carried are usually thrown in strings around the neck and over the shoulders. The string is tied in knots, leaving space enough for one hundred between each knot. This is done for convenience and rapidity of count, when received or paid out.

The value of this cash for use, as contrasted with the currency of other countries, fluctuates from day to day according to the supply and demand. The usual market value in most parts of the Empire, however, is the one thousandth part of a Mexican dollar, though twelve hundred are frequently realized by the lucky holder.

It must not be taken for granted that this currency is continually carried in much quantity about the person. It is kept in the coffer at the house, and the necessary quantity dealt out as occasion may require. It is a rare occurrence for foreigners to carry money about their person. The Chinese sometimes have a few silver dollars in a belt about their waist and underneath all their clothing, and perhaps a few cash for the purchase of some knick-knack that may come under their observation. But, usually, the foreigner's treasure is in the vault securely constructed in his house, or iron safe; whilst the Chinese, having melted the silver dollar and extracted all the alloy, put it into a mould called a shoe, (from its resemblance to a Chinese shoe) and carefully hoard it in the earth until needed in the transactions of business and commerce. This silver is called and known as sycee, and the shoes vary in value and size, from one tael to ten thousand taels.

The currency of China is of decimal denomination, like that of the United States, and divided into as many parts, though not of corresponding values. Thus, ten cash make a candarin, ten candarin make a mace, ten mace make a tael — the cash, candarin, mace, and tael, corresponding with the mill, cent, dime and dollar. One tael is equal in value to one dollar and forty-eight cents of the currency of the United States. Probably, if the United States dollar had no alloy, and like the tael, was pure silver, their values would correspond.

The currency of China, it has been supposed, was merely one of account, the only circulating medium being the copper cash, already referred to. This idea was prevalent, no doubt, because at the ports opened to foreign trade, no other denomination was obtained. But, the tael and the half tael, composed of pure silver, have recently come to the observation of foreigners at the north, in the vicinity of Pekin, with the Chinese character upon the nugget, declaring the value. Well informed Chinese merchants unquestionably have all along been aware of this, but true to the policy of their government, of withholding all information except what, from policy or accident, may have been wormed out of them, they studiously kept this fact to themselves.

Mexican dollars are used more than any other foreign coin. They reach China, principally, through England. There is not much gold coin in circulation. The Chinese do not like it as money. It does not pass at its par value, as denominated at the mint. When used in trade, it passes at a barter, like merchandise; and the Chinaman is loth to allow a greater equivalent than the market value of the metal, according to its weight. The Chinese melt the coin, and use the metal, after extracting the alloy, in various kinds of mechanism.

All the merchants of position and capital, employ a shroff. His principal duties are to shroff the money when received at his house, whether in the shape of coin or sycee. He stamps his name upon each piece of silver, be it a dollar or a lump of sycee, if the same is genuine : and it is then called *shroffed*, and passes without question. It is, however, a too common habit to nip or shave the shroffed piece of silver afterwards, as the same passes from hand to hand; and allowance therefor is required. Silver is a precious metal, and the quantity nipped or shaven off, be it ever so little, has a value. This practice gave rise to a Chinese saying, that "silver will stick to your fingers."

The Chinese land measure is divided into Maou, Foo-Haou, and Li — three maou being equal in quantity to one acre, as measured in the United States. The annual Imperial rent therefor, paid for the use of land, is about four dollars and fifty cents American currency, per acre. This ground rent can be paid by the native, in case of necessity, with the produce of the soil, as valued by the Te-paou of his district. It takes the place of the land tax as levied in the nations of the West, and is the only stated charge from the government which the occupier is compelled to pay throughout the year. If an unusual calamity occurs in the district, not occasioned by the people themselves, and causing unusual distress, the emperor has sometimes been pleased to remit a portion if not the whole of the rent. This clemency would seem in the eyes of the stranger, to be caused entirely by feelings of kindness, and generosity. The unfortunate and uneducated Chinese undoubtedly so view it. It would be the part of charity for the educated Chinese, as well as the historian of every country, so to view it. The times and circumstances, however, when and under which such kindness has been exhibited, indicates that it proceeds from a dread of the effects of famine and turbulence among the people; and philosophically calculating the cost to the Imperial exchequer of quelling an *emeute*, and coolly poising the scale as it balances between the rent and the outlay, the astute and cold-hearted prompter believes the throne of his majesty points to the latter, and the vermillion pencil straightway announces the result of this philanthropic deliberation. It is proclaimed at Pekin and in every provincial capital, in the largest sized hieroglyphics, upon sheets of yellow paper of mammoth size, and commanding every dweller in the "Middle Kingdom" and the Barbarians outside, to give ear and take heed of this most merciful condescension and goodness of their most august and kind-hearted Father.

In this spirit is it commonly received and read by the people; and lest its remembrance may quietly wear off and fade away from the memory, no convenient occasion to recal the event is lost by the small button Mandarins, who expatiate upon the theme, from generation to generation, until the pall of oblivion has encircled it forever.

These proclamations, no matter upon what subject, always end with the words "tremble and obey." The injunction is literally respected by the masses. They are uneducated. They learn to believe that the rulers must be obeyed. They do not stop to inquire into the authority, or the means at hand to enforce it. They are not versed in the maxims of government. They are never asked their views. They never vote. They do not discuss the doings of officials. They simply obey. They are the automatons of authority. They believe that, willing or unwilling, they are subordinate to the Mandarins, and that the "vermillion pencil" gives these officials the right and power to govern. With this, they associate in their minds the idea which is always kept prominent,— that the Emperor, on ascending the dragon throne, becomes more than a mere mortal, and possesses a divine right to wield the sceptre. This is sufficient. They make no further inquiry, and are passive slaves. Their desire and chief care is to keep out of the clutches of the Mandarins ; for they know the severe punishment that will be inflicted for disobedience.

The Chinese laws visit the offender with corporal punishment. Whoever sheds blood, or in committing a theft breaks an enclosure, must expiate the offence with his own blood — that is, his head is cut off. If he escapes, the law is cheated of its due. There are no pardons, no reprieves, no benefit of clergy, unless superinduced by bribery.

CHAPTER IX.

THE AVOCATIONS OF THE CHINESE.

THE Chinese are not naturally a fighting people. They prefer work and the peaceful avocations of trade. Whatever of fighting qualities they possess, comes from the Tartar blood.

If they are artisans, traders or merchants, they collect together in large villages and cities, the former more or less protected from external enemies by stockades and mud forts, and the latter, by high and thick stone walls. If they are farmers, instead of living in isolated farm houses, they huddle together in families of tens and twenties, and with as many tenements, and a suitable number of barns and out houses, dwell in unity and greater security. Their farms are a greater or less distance from their hamlet within the range of a mile, or three li — the equivalent of an English mile — and thither they daily repair to work the soil. Ditches usually are the lines of their possessions, and for aught that appears they live in harmony. If they are mere laborers — commonly called *coolies* — they do the carrying of burdens both in town and country. There are no carts, trucks or wagons, for the land conveyance of merchandise. It is borne, however light or ponderous, from and to the store houses, called in China *godowns*, by the coolies. They also take the place of the beast in the land conveyance of passengers who can afford it, and prefer riding to walking. The vehicle used is called in common parlance "a chair," and is known to foreigners as the Sedan or Palanquin. This mode of traveling by the officials and the opulent classes, has been in use in the East "from the time when the memory of man runneth not to the contrary." If they are born upon boats and vessels, as thousands and hundreds of thousands of them are, they are apt to continue in the same employment for want of a better, to the end of their lives. It has been said that one eighth of the entire population are born, live and die, on the waters. Their san-pans and luggers are used in the ports and and along the inlets of the coast, and far into the interior on the creeks and rivers, which meander the land in every direction, carrying passengers and luggage and merchandise. Large numbers of them are engaged in fishing, and frequently go off many miles from the coast. The Junks are the largest in size, and generally have three slender masts. This class of vessels is mostly engaged in the coasting trade along the whole extent of China, and not unfrequently extend the voyage, as far as Siam and Malacca. They move slow, and if it is to the countries just mentioned, one voyage suffices for the year. The owner is usually aboard as master or supercargo, and the profits made on the exchange of cargo frequently constitute a part of the freight-moneys or earnings of the vessel. It is not a strange occurrence for five thousand of these boats and vessels to be lying at the same time in the harbor of Shanghai. Well informed persons have sometimes reckoned the number as high as ten thousand, and have not been wide of the mark. It is amazing to behold the water carriages and small craft that congregate at and in the vicinity of the various ports, their number is so large, and apparently so full of business and employment. And then the number of persons aboard and the manner in which they live! An entire family is raised up and live on the same boat which one would fancy hardly large enough for the convenient accommodation of one person. There they cook, wash, sleep, and work, year after year, rear a numerous progeny, and have their poultry and ducks, their dog and cat, the same as if living on shore. If they want fish, they drop the hook or throw the net into the water, wherever the boat may happen to be, and in a trice catch enough for their meal. With fish they can secure their rice and the necessary quantity of vegetables; if not, they can sell a chicken or a duck or some eggs, and invariably procure what is indispensably requisite for their sustenance and comfort. Compared with the general mass of the people of civilized countries, their wants are few. Unaccustomed to the luxuries of wealth, they do not desire them. It is a part of the Divine economy that this is so; otherwise millions would starve, and violence and anarchy would necessarily prevail.

The national and political condition of the different regions of China varies strikingly, according to the peculiarities in their physical circumstances and the character of the viceroys sent from the chief seat of government, to rule over them.

The valley of the Yangtze river was the seat of

the Empire for many centuries, and that too, when its greatness and splendor eclipsed those of almost every other country. It was populous and wealthy, and avarice and ambition were attracted from afar by the fame of its wealth and splendor.

The long list of emperors who, for forty centuries at least, if not fifty-five, as some traditions have it, sat enthroned in the Celestial palaces of Nankin, these mighty potentates — the extent of their jurisdiction varying at different eras — very naturally might have expected that China, separated from other countries on the one hand by a vast ocean, and on the other by lofty mountains, and dense forests, and wide deserts, could rest secure from foreign conquest or dominion. The student of history finds much difficulty in forming a correct estimate of the character of these extraordinary monarchs. Their crimes, if viewed through the stereoscope of Christian morality, are written in too deep and legible characters to remain concealed. In the administration of justice, the general tenor of their lives are apparently marked by many virtues. Assiduous and impartial, yet subject to frightful fits of caprice and passion. Their charities were scattered with a liberal hand, and an unbounded concern at all times shown for the welfare of their people. Surrounded by the most ample means of licentious indulgence, yet as austere and free from censure as the rulers of other nations. Assuming to be the representative of heaven on earth, each surrounded himself with a halo of religious professions and zeal — such as it was — which he maintained through life, and which was cheerfully recognized by the myriads of people over whom he held sway. But the manifest exaggeration with which it was sometimes exhibited, and still more from its having been made an instrument of ambition and even of crimes, induce the suspicion if not belief, that there may have been beneath all this austerity, courtesy and kindness, a good deal of interested and hypocritical pretension.

CHAPTER X.

THE EMPIRE — THE EMPERORS — KIND OF GOVERNMENT — IMPERIAL ABODE — THE EXECUTIVE OFFICERS — THEIR REGALIA AND DUTIES — THE ARCHIVES.

THE country usually known as China, is divided into eighteen provinces. The Empire embraces these provinces, which constitute the main body of the Imperial Government, and also as dependencies those regions known as Corea, Mantchooria, Mongolia, Ili, Soongaria, East Toorkistan, Kokonor, Thibet, and numerous islands adjacent to the sea coast, the largest of which are Hainan, and Formosa. The two latter islands and Mantchooria are practically a part of the Empire, whilst the others do little more than profess a nominal allegiance. The area of this vast Empire covers 5,000,000 of square miles, nearly equal to one tenth of the habitable globe, with one third of the entire population, and is situated between the 18th and 56th parallels of north latitude, and the 70th and 144th degrees of east longitude, reckoning from Greenwich.

The population, according to the census taken by the Chinese has increased as follows :

    1757, . . . 190,348,328
    1780, . . . 277,543,434
    1812, . . . 361,693,179
    1841, . . . 413,457,311
    Last Census, 414,686,994

The Tepaous are the persons who take the census, and make their respective returns to the Governor of the Province, who forwards the same to the proper bureau at Pekin. The Tepaou is an officer of a small district in each town or city, whose chief business is to keep a record of the titles to land, note the change of ownership, and collect the land tax. This tax is the annual ground rent to the Emperor, the fee always remaining in him as the lord of the soil. There does not appear to be any inducement for the Tepaous to swell the number of people in his district.

The government of this great country centers in one person known in the English language as the Emperor, who calls himself the Son of Heaven, and accountable only to heaven for this stewardship. He professes to be guided by a code of laws which are composed of the rescripts and statutes of the Pure Dynasty. But his will is law to all who bow to his sceptre. His subjects view him as the father of the nation. In theory the government is patriarchal, but in practice it is despotic. He is supposed to rule as a father over his family, keeping in view only their good, and allowing the blessings of his government to fall gently upon all alike, like the dew of heaven. Clothing himself in the garb of the Holy of Holies, claiming to be the supreme pontiff on earth of the great God of the whole universe, he manages to invest his person and habitation with the most sacred character. No one out of his household approaches him except in the most reverential manner, and even those who are nearest to his person treat him with the most obsequious respect. It is a favor of priceless importance to the subject, if even allowed to enter the gates of the Imperial capital. He is kept at a distance from the person of the Emperor, for familiarity would dispel the awe and religious illusion that surrounds his person. To make secure from intrusion, the Imperial abode is within an inner circle of wall, the third from the outer one of the city. Within the periphery of the outer and second walls, the general mass of the people are allowed to dwell — within that of the second and the inner walls, the gentry and the wealthy. The Imperial abode is fitted up in the most gorgeous manner. It dazzles and bewilders, but does not charm the visitor who may have come from Western civilization to behold it. Though the grounds are covered with attractive fountains, and lakes, and cascades, and the buildings are of pompous size and gilded and decorated as dazzlingly as the most fanciful of painters could imagine, yet it is not elegant or beautiful. It is tawdry if not ridiculous,— the ornaments have too much of show and too little of grace. But all this gorgeousness attracts the attention of the Asiatics for whom it is intended, captivates their minds, and inspires them with all the awe and respect that is requisite to make them loyal subjects, and unyielding believers in the divinity of their august master. Therefore they do not hesitate, when entering into his presence, to humiliate themselves and kotow to his majesty by stooping the body three times in quick succession, and each time knocking the floor three times with the forehead, and thus making the nine prostrations. The subject who has enjoyed this favor is at once upon his return home a person of mark and respect among his neighbors. Like the poor bigot of Mohammedanism, who travels from afar to Mecca for the sole purpose of catching an indistinct glimpse of the coffin of his holy prophet, and then retraces his steps to his kindred and country with his faith burning brighter than ever, to receive their attention and enthusiasm, so with the loyal Chinaman who has traveled from his home perhaps in the far South, and been admitted into the inner circles of the city of Pekin, returns a warmer devotee, and inspired with renewed veneration for his celestial pontiff.

The Imperial mind, in the management of the government, is assisted by four ministers of state selected on account of their social position, education, and zealous attachment to the throne, who form the interior council chamber; they are the Cabinet officials, who are invested with the secrets of the Emperor, and have free access to his ear. Beneath them are Assistants, who constitute the principal council of state relative to such matters as may be laid before them.

For the transaction of the government business in detail there are six Boards, or Departments, namely, of Revenue, of Ceremonies, of Military Affairs, of Public Works, of Crimes, of Censors. There are executive officers appointed for the various Provinces, invested with the authority and dignity of Viceroys, and called Governor Generals, Governors, and Lieutenant Governors. The circuit of jurisdiction of these officers determines their official grade. If it extends over two or more Provinces, they are styled Governor Generals; if confined to one Province, over which there is no Governor General, then they are called Lieutenant Governors. In either case, they are the Emperor's substitute within their own Circuit, and are invested with regal power. Beneath these officers there are other local officials, styled Provincial Treasurer, Criminal Judge, and and Collector of the Gabel, or salt tax, whose circuits of jurisdiction are commensurate with the province.

Subordinate to these provincial officials there are other officers styled Toutais, or Intendants of Circuits, Cheheens or District Judges, Literary Chancellors, Military Commandants, Marine Prefects, and Tepaous, and whose jurisdiction embraces parts of the Province, and sometimes are circumscribed to the limits of a single city. In addition, there is a multitude of police, clerks of courts, secretaries, and executioners,— in short, the whole paraphernalia of an executive and administrative power.

All whose authority is undivided in its department in a single province, circuit, or district, from the Marine Prefect to the Governor General, are styled Mandarins, and are entitled to wear a button, of which there are nine grades, and which are as well the badge of official position, as of the exact grade, on the roll of distinction. The button, as it is called, is fastened to the official cap, on the outside, exactly at the center, of different colors according to the grade, of an oblong shape, and usually made from some precious stone.

The cap worn in cold weather, is made of felt, and in warm weather of straw, or very fine bamboo. It is of a conical shape, surmounted with a red or scarlet silk tassel, and a long feather of the peacock. These ornaments and the button, make an imposing head-dress. In addition, the Mandarin is clothed whenever he appears in public, with three, or more coverings of silk and satin, over the entire body, namely: the one next to the body, appropriately called the shirt; another over this, well wadded with cotton and extending to the knees, and appropriately called the petticoat,—another, over this, extending to the ankles, of the thickest silk crape, or satin, open in front, and fastened together with silk loops and cords; whilst over his feet and limbs are tightly drawn light colored silk stockings and drawers. All these several suits of apparel have much embroidery and are encircled with a girdle at the waist. Large and high-top satin boots are worn at all seasons, and in cold weather, very heavy and costly robes of fur. He is carried in a palanquin, borne by four coolies, and accompanied by his guards, the head one always carrying a large spread scarlet-colored umbrella, and the others, many silk banners. When he alights from or enters his palanquin, this cavalcade beat the gong, and halloo, so that all may take heed of the presence of the official and make way for him. The multitude *chin chin* him, as he passes along, that is, each person places the palm of the two hands together and raises and lowers them together three or four times, as an act of obeisance.

There is a board of officers at Pekin, whose duty it is to take note of all the important events in every province, in each month. At the end of every period of twelve months, commencing with the first of the year, this general note of events for the year is thoroughly scrutinized; and from it is culled whatever the board may deem important to mark the year in the continuous history of the country. This annual compilation is carefully and neatly written or printed on wooden type, strongly stitched or tied together, the seal of the examining board stamped upon the compilation, and then it is put in the place appropriated for its safe keeping. These annual compilations are the archives of the empire; and the mandarins assert that they extend back quite sixty hundred annual revolutions of the sun. It is admitted, however, that the compilation of events occurring before the transfer of the seat of government from Nankin to Pekin is not so full as of later times. It is supposed that many of the archives were then lost, but enough is preserved to give more than a mere outline of history. The student can find, at least, each decade of years.

CHAPTER XI.

QUALIFICATIONS OF THE MANDARINS — THE COURT LANGUAGE — OFFICIAL DELINQUENCY — ADMINISTRATION OF JUSTICE.

BY the laws of China, the Mandarins must be men of education, they must be well posted in the maxims and philosophy of Confucius Mencius and others of their sages, and intimately acquainted with the rescripts and statutes of the Empire. To obtain this information requires much patience and assiduity, and many years of attentive study. The student, as with us of the Western hemisphere, commences the great task when young, and at manhood applies, through the literary chancellor of his district, for the privilege of undergoing an examination before the established Board of Examiners at Pekin. When he receives their permit to repair to the capital, he sets out upon the journey with as much solemnity of thought and feeling, as if about to enter upon the profession of the priesthood. Upon his arrival at Pekin the applicant is assigned a room by himself, in quarters prepared by the government. Here he is kept for three weeks, preparatory for the examination; and during that time is forbidden all intercourse with any person whatever. No person is allowed to enter his apartment except the coolie who waits upon him. He partakes of his meals by himself. The reason for this strict *surveillance* is to preclude all temporary knowledge. He is thus prevented from availing himself of the learning of any friend at his elbow. If he passes through the ordeal successfully, it is because of his thorough erudition acquired before reaching the capital. When the examination is progressing in the great hall of examination, the students are not allowed to mingle. This is an effectual interdict against one friend aiding another. At night they are returned to their respective rooms. All these precautions are in force till the examination is finished; if he is successful, the Board report him to the consideration of the Emperor, and the vermillion pencil marks the character that confers upon him the button of a mandarin. He is then eligible to official position.

These examinations occur triennially. The applicant for the permit is frequently refused; and when gratified in this particular, is often pronounced unqualified to become a Mandarin by the board at Pekin, and disappointed and usually heart-broken, retraces his steps to his home, if he does not commit suicide on the way. To be eligible even for the permit, it is necessary that he should not only be able to read and talk the language of the imperial court, but he must be able to write it with fluency and perspicuity; this accomplishment in other countries is thought of minor importance, and to read and write merely — especially to write — but a short advance on the highway of knowledge. In Chinese scholarship, however, it is otherwise. This court language, or Mandarin as it is usually called, is the only language that is known and used alike all over the Empire. The laws and rescripts of government, in order to be uniform and certain at all points of the commonwealth, and alike understood, are expressed by the same characters and of the same meaning. Those who are charged with the execution of these laws and rescripts, must of necessity be familiar with the language. The language of the mass of the people is unlike in the different provinces, and hence the dialect taught to the child illy qualifies him for the post of a mandarin. To learn the meaning of these symbolical characters, and then to possess the ability to unite them is not, as in Western nations, the work of months, but of years. Neither is the student favored with free schools, but is taught at his own expense by some private tutor or in some private school. When, however, he has thoroughly mastered the language and become familiar with the laws and institutions of his country, the maxims of government, the precepts and instructions of Confucius and Mencius, the religious dogmas of Buddha, and the elementary principles of right and wrong — and above all been accepted by the Board of Examination — then he has achieved a prize in the great lottery of life. He is decorated with the first button, and enters upon official life. He now begins to travel that narrow path which is sure, if he takes care not to make a false step, to lead him to wealth and fame.

It is from such a class of men that the high ministers of state, Governors, Judges, Magistrates and Chancellors, are selected. It is with such men that the representatives of foreign powers come in contact. Such erudition, united with the intellectual ability and persevering energy to acquire it, would be formidable in any country; and is especially so in a country where its language would be deemed an enigma if not a myth, by the people of other lands, if history and tradition did not develope the stubborn fact that this identical language was the first spoken, if not the first written language on the earth. Chronicles wholly detached from the fabulous epoch of twenty four thousand years, produce the conviction that these characters and hieroglyhics were used to express the same symbols with the same idea and meaning, away back in the first dawn of time.

There is as much jostling, however, among the Mandarins to get this and that seal of office, as there is among applicants for official position in Europe or America. They have their intrigues, and the ins and outs wrestle as much with each other. Three years is the usual duration of an office, though not necessarily terminating then, as the seal is held at the will of the Emperor. Usually, there is apparent concord among those in the seats of authority. If the Board of Censors lodges a complaint in the imperial ear, it has come up to the capital through some other source than the high officials of the province. The principal reason for this, as rumor hath it, is the sensitiveness so prevalent among all upon the subject of official delinquency or dereliction of duty.

They do not seek occasion to *belie*, as they express it, the well beloved and right trusty servants of the Son of Heaven. Human nature is subject to short comings, they say, and the mandarin's walk may not at all times be as straight as a line can be drawn between two points. So far from evincing a disposition to even cast a slur upon each other's conduct, they are too apt to go a great way to cover up any alleged malversation. The cause of this aversion to fault finding is because, as the Chinese aver, the mandarins believe in the maxim that "those who live in glass houses should not throw stones."

Most of the complaints, as talked over by the people among themselves, are against those mandarins who hold the courts. These magistrates are charged with corruption — daily corruption. Indeed, it has become so common in many localities, that a Chinaman who has been wronged, in ninety-nine cases out of an hundred, prefers to let the wrong go unpunished than to make the matter known at the magistrate's office. If a Chinaman is indebted to another Chinaman, he is very apt to go scot free, such is the disinclination to prosecute. For, whenever a Chinaman lodges a complaint, civil or criminal, the first thing he is required to do, is to pay a liberal douceur to some one in attendance, under the false pretext that the same is to pay the necessary expenses in court, for the police officers, and for writing out the proceedings.

The court is held by one person, styled "Cheheen." There is no jury — there are no associates. There is, practically, no appeal. The law allows of an appeal in certain cases, but there does not appear to be any way to get the case before the Appellate Court, which again is held by the Criminal Judge of the province without associates or jury. The appellant cannot himself, as in some other countries, take the case to the court above, nor can he compel a true return of the whole case by the court below, without virtually making a complaint against it, or, in other words, impugning the judicial capacity of the Cheheen; for, in Chinese law it is assumed that the Cheheen is perfectly familiar with the maxim of justice that is applicable to the case, and therefore, if he has in fact made a wrong decision, it has emanated from impure motives. If then, an appeal is made, and the decision is overruled, the appellant incurs the displeasure of the Cheheen, and will soon feel it to his great cost and detriment. If the appeal is dismissed, he is mulcted heavily to pay the numerous wily hangers-on about the purlieus of justice. If it is a case of indebtedness, the creditor really gets nothing. Besides, to prevent false accusations, the party who fails to substantiate the complaint is always fined or otherwise punished. Many instances can be cited to illustrate the truth of these observations of Chinese jurisprudence. One or two may now suffice.

CHAPTER XII.

THE JUNK CASE — CIVIL SIDE OF COURT.

AN owner of a junk borrowed upon a note in the nature of a mortgage on the vessel, two thousand taels. A quarter of the purchase money was to be repaid in one month, and time allowed for the payment of the balance. When the pay day came, the purchaser did not meet the payment. The interest, which was lawfully agreed upon at twelve per cent. per annum, there being no usury law, remained unpaid also. After much unsuccessful effort to tease payment, and the whole amount having become due, the money lender very reluctantly unbosomed himself to the district magistrate. The Secretary politely requested a few taels as an entrance fee to the Cheheen. The Messenger was too unwell to announce this suitor for justice until a package of one hundred Mexican dollars was handed to him.

The police officer was too much worn out with the heat and travel of the previous day, to undertake to find the debtor, and did not feel as if it was possible to enter upon this new undertaking, until the suitor had also quietly laid upon *his* stool "another hundred." These requirements complied with, the suitor was informed that he could then " go and return on some other day." He left and did return " on some other day " three weeks afterwards, when he found his debtor in prison.

The suitor was now informed that the debtor not only denied the justice of the claim, but insisted that the suitor was guilty of forgery — that the *seal* to the writing or note was not genuine. By law it is necessary that all writings shall not only have the mark or sign manual but also the *seal;* and hence all Chinese of the slightest respectability have their private seals of different devices.

This is necessary because of the scarcity of surnames, and the necessity of so many persons using the same. Indeed, those of the same family are all known by one name, unless it is arbitrarily changed.

Well, in this case the suitor was dumbfounded. He, however, after the fashion of the Chinese, reassured himself by adding largely to the previous douceurs, and petitioned the Cheheen to meet his debtor face to face with witnesses.

After the lapse of one month, he had this privilege, and his debtor confronted him with what he claimed as his genuine seal. It was different from the one upon the note, and the Cheheen sternly admonished the suitor of his delicate situation and the necessity of "clearing up the matter." To add to his confusion, the man in custody was not the person with whom the trade was in fact made, though of the same name and residence, and yet, as it appeared from the evidence of the witnesses, he was the true owner of the junk in question. One of them declared that he sold to the prisoner the identical spars that were used for the masts. The suitor did not know what to do. If the matter was dropped then, the Cheheen, according to custom, would bamboo him at least; that is, the Court would sentence him to receive some forty or fifty blows of the bamboo stick upon the *naked back*, and the sentence would be immediately carried into execution, and he would lose his debt. So he asked for time — just what the Court expected — and a future day was named for another sitting in the case, and the debtor remanded to prison. As the suitor was about leaving this temple of justice, some by-stander intimated to him that he had better compromise the matter in some way with the stubborn debtor, if he could do so conveniently. This intimation was sufficient. He received from his debtor five hundred and sixty-four taels, corresponding exactly with the total amount of douceurs, and consented in writing that the debtor might be let out on bail given for his reappearance whenever summoned by the Cheheen.

Once upon a time thereafter, these two Chinese met in an opium shop, each to drown his sorrow;— the suitor, because he never could come across the person who really borrowed the money; and the debtor, because he had been compelled to pay two thousand taels for which he had never received an equivalent. The opium shop disclosed the fact that the debtor was twice *bambooed* by the Cheheen, because he so stubbornly denied the debt; and through the influence of friends had escaped the further punishment if he had admitted the debt in open court, by paying over the two thousand taels and full interest, and which, until this accidental meeting, he supposed had gone into the pocket of the suitor.

This was a proceeding on the civil calendar of the court.

CHAPTER XIII.

THE WIDOW WOMAN. — CRIMINAL SIDE OF COURT.

THE following case may be cited as having occurred on the criminal calendar of this astute, if not impartial tribunal.

One day a middle-aged, widowed woman appeared at the bureau of the Secretary, and complained that a Chinaman had stolen her only child,— a girl of fourteen years of age, — taken her to a neighboring province, and sold her. It was a case of kidnapping.

She was told that it was necessary, under the law, for some male to appear in court with her, as her next friend, as no female could be suitor in her own name. She retired. In a few days she re-appeared in company with her brother. The accused was a well known Chinese merchant, and not poor. The widow was very politely reminded of this by the kind and affable Secretary, and some surprise evinced that he should be guilty of so horrid a crime. The widow was not dull to comprehend, and at once began to count out the dollars, thinking that the Secretary would say " enough," as each changed ownership. In this she was mistaken, as the last one she had passed out of her hands, and the Secretary had not said " enough." On the contrary, he asked for more, assigning as a reason, that the punishment for the alleged crime was severe — no less than the loss of the *head* — that the accused had plenty of *sycee*, (pure silver,) and she had laid her damages as high as two tens of thousands of taels. She excused herself and retired again. One moon, however, had not more than passed, and she waited upon the Secretary the third time in quest of justice. Now, the Secretary said " enough," her petition to the Cheheen was duly prepared and signed, and she was told when to come again with her brother. At the expiration of a fortnight she and her brother confronted the kidnapper in court.

The accused had been arrested but not thrown into prison, being connected with a foreign house, satisfactory bail had been given for his forthcoming at the required time. He denied the charge, and claimed that it was an attempt on the part of the widow to extort money.

In Chinese courts, each party, as well as the witnesses, are always examined by the judge, and the person under examination kneels and bows the head to the floor, and remains in this posture, till the examination is concluded. So it was done in this case. The accused trembled like an aspen leaf,— so much so — that he hardly knew what answer to make when asked if he had ever seen the young girl. Unwittingly he admitted that he had once seen her; and though he attempted to parry off the many questions that this admission suggested to the mind of the inquisitor, yet he came lamely off.

The Cheheen robed in full dress, the emblems of punishment — such as bamboo sticks and chains and cords and axes — and on every side, plenty of executioners and policemen at hand to do the bidding of their master, for the nonce disconcerted him, and he finally, while stoutly denying the charge, stated that at the urgent request of her mother, he had taken some charge of the girl, and for her good, sent her to a friend a few *li* into the interior. To test the truth of this part of the story, as the Cheheen remarked, he was asked how much time he wanted to return the girl to her mother. He replied that it was one hundred and twenty *li* (equal to the distance of forty English miles.) The Court allowed eight days for the production of the missing girl, and he again gave satisfactory bail for his appearance in court at the designated time. The young girl returned to her mother one day, surprised that she should have sent for her so soon, as she was quite contented, but was hushed by the widow telling her how nicely she had planned to get into her clutches the accused Chinaman, who it turned out had merely been acting as a guardian of the girl, and that too at the earnest solicitation of her mother. But because he would not occasionally make her a *cumshaw*, that is a gift, of a few dollars, she adopted this course to squeeze him roundly. Flattering as she now thought the case to be, in the sequel she learned that the court did not think she was entitled to recover any damages, as the accused had done nothing wrong; but that she had shown herself a good and loyal subject in bringing the case to the attention of the proper authorities; and especially so, as she had done this at her own expense. It was not long after that she met the accused in the street, and importuning him for some pecuniary help received for a reply, that the big fish had nearly eaten him up, as he was forced to pay to the secretary one thousand taels; and, as he had till then supposed, as smart money to go into her ill gotten purse. She hastened once more to the Secretary, and got for an answer, that the affair was finished, and it was now her duty, as a good and loyal subject, to go home and quietly attend to her own business.

CHAPTER XIV.

RAILROADS. — COURIERS. — FORMALITIES. — THE YAMUNS.

THERE are no railroads nor telegraphic wires in China. The speed of ordinary traveling is slow, and there is no general system of Chinese mail conveyance. Between large neighboring cities in some localities there is a mail communication kept up by individual enterprise, and letters and news carried for a trifling compensation. An hundred miles is regarded as a long journey. When a mandarin is passing along, he is preceded by a herald who warns the inhabitants of the approach of the magnate, by the beating of gongs and the explosion of fire crackers. If the official is in a sedan, his guards walk ahead, the foremost carrying a scarlet umbrella — if he is in a boat, the same is known as a mandarin boat from its size and make, and an umbrella is stuck on the top of it. State communications are carried by special couriers, whose speed of travel is greater or less according to the importance of the communication and the rank of the officials between whom it passes. If to or from the Emperor, it is the flying courier who goes, as the Chinaman would say, "with lightning speed." He rides on horseback with relays at every thirty li, or ten English miles. Usually, the courier is relieved at the expiration of every hundred li, but the packet, carefully folded in a roll covered with scarlet silk and securely tied at each end and in the middle with silk ribbons, is constantly on the way till it has reached its destination. If from the Emperor it is written with the "vermilion pencil," and the officer to whom it is addressed meets it "beyond the outer gate" of the city, places it upon a table, chin chins it, and then causes it to be removed to his Yamun or palace, where it is very gravely unrolled and its contents ascertained after it has "lain in state" a sufficient length of time for other local officers, who wear the button of a mandarin, to come and chin-chin.

Every thing of a public character is attended with great formality. Indeed there is so much importance attached to formality, that it is the sole business of the Board of Rites and Ceremonies at Pekin, to make and prescribe rules and regulations for the carrying out of this maxim of government. If any public document or communication to, or passing between officers of the state, lacks the prescribed formality, the same is not received. Let the subject be of ever so trifling importance, the communication must have the impress of the official seal; and not only that, but the impress must be made exactly at the prescribed place and on the proper colored paper, either red or yellow, according to the subject or business; and then it must be slid into a red envelope left wholly open at one end and closely fitted; and then this must be carefully put into another and larger envelope securely pasted together and having the impress of the seal on the outer envelope in three different places, and so made as to cover each fold. The outer envelope must also be of the prescribed size, which is graduated, from twelve inches in length and six inches in breadth, to twenty-four by twelve, according to the rank of the officer.

So with the Yamuns or palaces, sedans and boats. Every Yamun in the empire, of the same official grade, is built in a similar fashion and of a similar size. There are three courts, two outer and one inner. If an officer, native or foreign, is approaching, a salute of three guns is always fired off in the outer court, accompanied with music. The guards of the Yamun, form in parallel lines facing each other, in the first inner court which the visitor enters, and between which lines he passes into the second inner court, where he alights from his sedan, and is greeted with a chin chin from the occupant of the Yamun, standing under a crimson canopy, and to whom the visitor chin chins in return for the compliment. The visitor is then escorted through narrow passages and galleries to a public reception room where, among other chairs, there is one more elevated than the others, with two seats beneath a red colored canopy, and to one of which he is introduced, the Chinese officer taking the other and on the right of the visitor, the left seat being, according to Chinese etiquette, the post of preference, instead of the right as in Western countries. The visitor having finished the business which called him there, and intimated his intention to retire, he is very politely, (no matter how exciting or unpleasant may have been the business that occasioned the interview,) invited to partake of refreshment consisting of wines, cakes and tea. It is regarded as a violation of etiquette to decline the invitation, and therefore it is always accepted even if only for a moment. The visitor is then conducted to the refreshment room, surrounded by the guards of the Yamun as he passes along; and having finished there as soon as he pleases, (etiquette conferring this privilege) he returns to his sedan and leaves the Yamun and its various courts with the same ceremony that he entered it. If he had come on foot, instead of being carried in a sedan by four bearers, it would have been a violation of the code of ceremonies for the governor, or whatever his official appellation, to have received him. It would be equally regarded as a violation of the regulations for the governor to make an official visit, or even to move along the public street, on foot, and what is singular he would be the laughing-stock of the populace.

CHAPTER XV.

CHINESE PECULIARITIES. — POLYGAMY.

THE Chinese are a peculiar race. Their habits and customs are *sui generis*. They are wholly like themselves, and wholly unlike everybody and everything else. Their disposition, and their mode of thought and action, are different from the rest of mankind. In the usual daily routine of life they are stoical, yet capable of gushing, overwhelming passion. They reverse the maxim of not deferring till to-morrow what can be done to-day, and act as if whatever can be done to-day can be done just as well to-morrow. They are never in a hurry, for the sun, they say, will come again in the east. They are superstitious, and are slowly, if ever persuaded, to deviate from the beaten walk of their ancestors. Believers in Buddhism, they have as a nation no faith in the divinity or doctrines of Jesus of Bethlehem. They are vain but frugal. They are industrious from necessity. They are very fond of trade, and always ready to barter whatever they may have. They have an abundance of low cunning, and many of their number are endowed with a far-seeing sagacity. They will cheat a foreigner if they can, and consider it a virtue to do so; and it is not far from the truth to say that many of them will steal if they cannot cheat. They believe in the propriety of polygamy, and practise it. The law tolerates the man in having as many women belonging to his person under his own roof, as he may be pleased to have; but if either, or the issue, are not taken care of, he forfeits his head to the government. Hence, he is apt to be careful of his conduct on this point. It is usual for a Chinaman who is well off, to have two wives, as they are called; and it is not a very extraordinary occurrence for a wealthy man to have six "*wife.*" The word as used in the English language, is not, however, significant of the true meaning of this transaction. In China, the "wife" is the woman who is first united to the man by the usual marriage ceremonies, and supposed to be of equal condition. Whilst she lives, she is always entitled by law to share the bed and board of her husband, and is the mistress of all the other women whom he may legally take to himself. She is at the head of the household on the female side. The other women are subordinate and of inferior condition, not united to the male head of the household by the usual rites of matrimony, and therefore are what is known in the English sense as concubines. They, as well as their children, are legally required to work and to do their share towards the common maintenance of the whole family, according to their condition and ability. The Chinese say that the additional woman is not taken without the consent of the wife, and that the harmony of the family is never disturbed by these domestic arrangements.

CHAPTER XVI.

HOW THE CHINESE GET THEIR WIVES — THE MARRIAGE CEREMONY.
THE MARRIAGE FEAST.

THE Chinese marriage ceremony is unique. To begin, the courting is done through a third person. A Chinaman who wants a wife employs some person — usually a female — to look out for a suitable match. This go-between usually belongs to a class who follow this business. She is therefore generally well informed of the marriageable women in her neighborhood at least, and their qualities, and the cost of getting them. The man must always pay a greater or less price to the parents, which is claimed as a recompense for the loss of her services, and the marriage outlay. The price varies according to the attraction of the woman, and the quality of her condition. The price ranges from five to ten hundred taels. It is said, that ten thousand taels of sycee is often left with the parents. The wooer commits himself and his future domestic peace and happiness entirely to the good sense, tact, and judgment of the go-between. It is pretended, that the wooer never indicates his choice, or knows, or even has seen to recognize, his partner in life. The go-between at once commences her work, and having made her selection, discloses the business to the parent with as much *non chalance* as she would open a negotiation for any article of produce or merchandise. She informs him of the character and pecuniary condition of the wooer, and commonly, after much chaffering, settles the price for the young lady. After this is paid, the time for the marriage is fixed. This ceremony takes place at the residence of the groom. On the morning of the day designated for this ceremony to begin, the wooer sends the " wedding chair " and an escort to the house of the parents, for his betrothed. In this she is brought to the groom's residence. The " wedding chair " is a large sized sedan covered with scarlet silk, and the bride is hidden from the view of the spectators as she passes along the highway. Ahead of her is the escort, consisting of some twenty to thirty persons, with music and fire-crackers, to warn the people to stand apart so that the bridal cortege may pass by, and to drive off any evil spirit that may be lurking near. Behind her follow the marriage gifts of her parents, and among which are always her bed and bedding. Arrived at her new home she is conducted to the bridal chamber, where she is left by herself and to her own thoughts. Neither party has recognized the other. They are strangers. There is an idol in a corner of the chamber, and she *chin-chins* it for virtue, plenty and felicity. She occupies this apartment for a season, varying from one to three days. She is not clothed in white, for that color is the symbol of mourning. She dresses as may be her taste, giving heed to the caprice of the Priest. In the meantime, the groom is at his devotion in another room. On the evening of the next day, attended by the priest and near relatives, the parties are for the first time brought into each other's presence; and kneeling together in front of an altar, with the left hand of the bride in the right hand of the groom, they *chin chin* the god of Matrimony. After a few minutes they return to their separate apartments, and do not again see each other till they meet at the table of the " marriage feast." This occurs on the following evening, or the third evening succeeding the arrival of the bride. The table is loaded with meats, cake and fruit, and decorated with a profusion of flowers in bunches and festoons. The invited guests are assembled around the table. The groom and bride having again knelt together at the altar, and jointly begged the consent of the god of matrimony to their union as man and wife, and the priest having announced a favorable response, they now for the first time appear in public as such, by entering the feast room together. They advance to the head of the table. The groom puts a gold ring into a small cup containing wine, and having sipped the wine passes the cup to the bride, who imitates his example. The priest then receives the cup, and whilst holding it, the groom withdraws the ring from the wine and places it on the third finger of the left hand of his bride. They are now husband and wife; and according to the laws of the Empire an indissoluble knot has been tied, which nothing but death can unloose. The laws do not tolerate divorce for any cause whatever. The marriage feast now proceeds, and the costly viands detain the company to a late hour.

CHAPTER XVII.

HOLIDAYS.— HOW TIME IS RECKONED.

THE Chinese have their festivals, amusements, and games. The four days at the beginning of each new year for the lower classes, and thirty for the gentry; the opening of each of the four seasons — winter, spring, summer and autumn; the annual cleaning of the graves of their ancestors in the month of March; the annual days set apart to *chin chin* the Sun, Moon, Wind, Rain, Earth, and Water; these are holidays, and all can rest from their labors. They do not use the seven days, or the four weeks, or the names of the twelve months, or reckon from them as in Western nations. They divide time into years, moons and days. For the year they reckon from the first year of the reign of the Emperor for the time being; for the moon, from the first to the twelfth moon of the year; for the day, from the first to the thirtieth of the moon. As for the parts of a day, hour, minute or second, they are used by the uneducated as of the morning or evening in a general sense. Twelve hours constitute a day reckoned from midnight. Each hour is subdivided into ninety-six *kih*, or eighths — each eighth being equal to fifteen minutes Western time. At the expiration of every sixty moons they intercalate an additional moon, to complete the cycle of time. In this way, they nearly agree with Europe and America in the computation of intervals of duration from age to age. This intercalation, is the result of astronomical observation, like the adding of an extra day every fourth year to the month of February; or like the adding or subtracting of a day by the mariner in the ship's log, according as the ship may be going west or east, as he crosses the 180th degree of longitude in the Pacific ocean.

CHAPTER XVIII.

AMUSEMENTS. — TEA HOUSES. — OPIUM. — DINNER PARTIES.

THOUGH the general mass of the people do not have as many days of rest as in some other countries, yet their places of amusement are open daily. In all large cities there are one or more public places of amusement, consisting of theatrical representations and jugglery. The temples usually furnish a suitable room or court, and the net profits probably go into the purse of the priesthood. The charge of admittance is the mere trifle of one cash, equal in value to the tenth part of an American cent. Thousands of idlers, therefore, habitually frequent these resorts of pleasure. The gentry are accustomed to hire the "whole house;" and then only those who have been invited, can gain admittance. A foreigner soon tires. The language is unintelligible, the music of the shrill fifes and clarinets and of the rumbling gongs, is too piercing and heavy for the ear, and the jostling and odor of the immense crowd is too hard and unpleasant, to induce him very often to repeat the visit. But the natives enjoy the fun with rapture. They are also passionately fond of games from their youth to old age, and all classes, both ashore and afloat, participate. One can seldom pass along the street, without seeing the children at their plays of dice and quoits; or along the bund or quay, without noticing on the deck of many a junk and boat some of the people sprawled thereon, at the game of matching dice. It is the same in the houses of public refreshment, called "tea houses," because tea is the beverage usually called for and supplied in those places. If a Chinaman desires to get drunk (and he is frequently so inclined if he has an extra cash or two,) he goes to another class of restaurants, and having ordered and been served with his money's worth of opium and the pipe in which to smoke it, he reclines upon a bunk with a stand beside it, and takes a whiff of the charming herb at his pleasure. If he belongs to the class of wealthy persons, whose number is legion, instead of repairing to a public house, he retires to his own, and there has his games and his opium. If fond of company, he entertains his acquaintances and friends at dinners which come off at the close of the day, and extend far into the night. His wife and concubines do not participate, as the males and females, especially among the upper classes, do not mess together at the same table. His wife, however, is allowed to entertain at dinner, but ladies only are her guests. Her entertainment is equally long and as delicious, but attended with more parade.

On these occasions, the ladies vie with each other not only in respect to their personal appearance and the style and beauty of their dresses, as is customary in many other countries, but also in the variety and number of dresses used at the entertainment.

It is the fashion at these dinners to have many courses of meats, and pastry, and desserts. With the change of every course, the company retires, and reappears in a different dress. Each guest has brought her wardrobe, and her servants arrange, in the dressing room, in advance of the first sitting at the table, the several dresses and ornaments that her misstress is to put on, from one course to the other, during the entertainment. As the guest does not know the number of courses to be served, she orders at random a number of silk, satin, and crape dresses to be ready, taking care to have it large enough. Sometimes she makes a miss, and then receives the triumphant smiles of those who guessed nearer the mark; and the hostess politely expresses her gratification that the feast has surpassed the expectation of her kind guest.

The ladies do not attend the public amusements, nor are those of the upper classes allowed to walk in the public streets. They remain at home, and there have their amusements and games. When they go out, they are carried in the sedan, and are screened from the observation of the people outside. It is in this way, say the Chinese, that the ladies are protected from insult and injury, and relieved of the stare of the vulgar and impertinent. The true reason undoubtedly is, to keep the mind and heart at home. For there, it is claimed, the rich man's wife enjoys all the luxuries of the land, and whiles away the time amid music, flowers, and embroidery.

CHAPTER XIX.

THE VARIOUS TRADES. — ROADS. — HOUSES. — CATTLE. — MODE OF DOING BUSINESS.— COOLIES.

THE various trades of Western civilization are also to be found in China. The mechanism is more primitive, and it is not carried to that degree of perfection, or applied to as many uses. The genius of invention is a stranger to this old country, and there does not appear to be any demand from the people for improvement. The plow and drag are the same as used centuries ago. They care not for the fanning mill, and prefer the sieve and basket to separate the chaff from the wheat. They can still rake the straw and grass by hand, and use the sickle and snath, as in olden time. The shoemaker prefers the straight awl, though he does not use pegs to fasten the sole to the upper leather. The barber likes the broad-bladed and straight-handled razor, though he shaves the top and back of the head as well as the face. The tailor cannot or will not use the yard stick, and plies the shears and goose upon the principle that resemblances are realities. He prides himself upon being a good copyist, and insists that a coat, pantaloons, or vest, bearing the resemblance of the pattern is in reality of the same finish and durability. An important step will have been taken in the advancement of human progress and enlightenment, when the populations of this quarter of the globe shall have been made conscious that old ideas are fast being supplanted by new developments, and that the world of humanity is moving forward instead of backwards.

The bible and the ship, the missionary and the merchant, have accomplished much in this direction. The civilization of Christian countries follows in the wake of their commerce, and Paganism is humbled in its presence.

Sheep are raised in central and northern China. The wool is long and coarse, and the mutton is excellent. They are of the same class that abounded in New England forty years ago. It is customary to use the skin with the wool unpicked, for clothing in cold weather. Wood is scarce and always brings a high price, and is sold by the weight or bundle, equal in price to about twenty-five Mexican dollars per English cord. The people, therefore, in lieu of having a fire to warm themselves, are compelled to have recourse to clothing, and increased in quantity from time to time, as the weather becomes colder, and decreased as the weather becomes warmer. January and February are the coldest months, July and August are the warmest months. The thermometer rises in many parts of the country to $102°$ Fahrenheit, and goes as low as $30°$ above zero. This is especially so in all that portion lying below the Yellow river. In the northern part of China the thermometer falls below zero in winter.

China abounds in goats. The people are not partial to the meat, but are fond of the milk. They have short horned and small size bullocks and cows, and also the water buffalo. They have horses, but it is unusual for the people to use them. Military officers appear on horseback, and, in the north of China, a two wheeled vehicle without springs, a mere cart, is drawn by horses when used in traveling. At other times it is drawn by oxen, and one ox usually suffices. It is a common occurrence to see only one ox harnessed to a plow. In each case the ox is driven by a rein attached to a ring fastened to the nose. But over most all of China, the sedan is the traveling vehicle, and is carried by two or four coolies, who travel at the rate of four or five miles an hour. The roads are narrow. They are mere footpaths of only sufficient width for two sedans to pass together. These roads are from four to six feet wide. The streets in the cities are of a similar width, and are usually paved with heavy, flat, slabs of granite. Underneath there is a small drain that empties into one or more canals or natural streams of water, which extend through the city and outside walls. The population is dense in the inhabited localities. The people dislike isolation, and every house, shop, store, and tenement, seems to overflow with living humanity. The lower classes wear but little clothing. Cooking of some kind is continuous from morning till night, all over the city. Oil is used instead of lard or butter, and the air is full of an undesirable aroma. This, together with the smell of decayed vegetables, garbage, and other offensive matter, makes a very unpleasant atmosphere for the foreigner. If there were no sites of land alloted for the exclusive occupancy of foreigners outside of the walls, a residence at any of the ports opened by the treaties would be intolerable. As it is, the foreign commercial business is mostly transacted in the house, called *hong*, of the merchant in the foreign settlement; and whoever has occasion to go into the native city, returns as soon as he can accomplish his errand.

In all marts of trade, the coolies are the beasts of burden. They work singly and in pairs, to an indefinite number. On their back and shoulders is carried all the merchandise and produce. There are no drays or wheelbarrows to divide this labor. No matter what is to change position, the services of the coolies are required. The heaviest machinery and the largest spars are carried by them. Their number is legion, and when at work, they make the town ring with the song of "Ha-Ko, Ho-Ka," as they jog along the street. There are no sidewalks, the street or road is the walk over which footmen pass.

The hiring of Chinese coolies to go to the West Indies, has engaged the attention of traders. Lately for many years, the labor of the coolie has been contracted for a term of years, and the coolie taken to the West Indies. Six to eight dollars per month and board, and the promise to return him to China, have been the usual terms upon which the coolie has consented to go. But so much dissatisfaction has attended the adventure — arising from a misconception of it by the coolie as well as the alarm of his friends — that the business has grown into disfavor. These laborers are undoubtedly well adapted for work in hot latitudes, and their labor would be remunerative on sugar, rice and cotton plantations.

CHAPTER XX.

THE REBELS — TAEPING WANG.

It is now full thirteen years since the Rebellion first showed its head in the vicinity of Canton. The Coolie boy whom Father Roberts taught and meant to christianize, has become the Mohammed of 1862; and, enthroned in his heavenly Yamun at Nankin, under the address of "Taeping Wang," dictates to hordes of followers. It is believed that there are in all the provinces at least one million of armed men enrolled under his banners. They are led in different directions to the four points of the compass under four general chiefs, styled Northern King, Eastern King, Southern King, Western King, and have overrun three-fourths of the heart of China. They have laid under heavy contribution of life and property hundreds of villages and thousands of hamlets, and with fire and knife desolated the country. It is usual for them to kill the old people and the young children, and press into their service the middle aged of both sexes. They are courageous and cruelly vindictive, and having been engaged so long in this business of war, they now have no inclination to return to the honest avocations of peace.

Taeping Wang claims to be divine, in the Christian sense. The Emperor claims also to be the representative of heaven on earth. But the rebel chief is not content with simply holding that position. He takes a loftier flight, and insists that he is the brother of Jesus Christ, and now daily takes his authority and inspiration from God our father. The Emperor knows not the man of Calvary or his inspired tenets. He is more familiar with Confucius. Not so Taeping Wang. He is a believer in the divinity of Christ. He observes the Sabbath. He and his household repeat the Lord's prayer morning and evening, and recognize the ten commandments substantially, though if half of what I hear is true, very imperfectly observe them; but he demands that all persons shall acknowledge him as divine, and commissioned to rule the earth, both temporally and spiritually. Because of this quasi recognition of the Christian religion, no doubt many at first thought the rebellion, if successful, would be the entering wedge to the evangelization of the "Flowery Kingdom." Hence the rebels at the outset had much sympathy, but as the aspirations of their chief leak out the tide ebbs in another direction, and now both merchant and missionary come nearer together in their estimate of the intellectual and moral character of these long-haired Asiatics. The result is that foreign troops (British and French) are aiding the Imperial authorities to finish the rebellion. Already several battles have been successfully fought near the port of Shanghai, and the probability is that these efforts will be renewed until peace is restored to the native population in that part of the Empire, at least.

The Taepings claim that they wish to unseat the present Imperial government because it is Tartar, and instead found a pure Chinese dynasty, and transfer the seat of authority to Nankin, the old capital when ruled by emperors of Chinese descent, centuries ago.

The distracted condition of the country has been very injurious to commerce. There has been much risk and difficulty in introducing foreign merchandise into the interior, and transporting the teas and silk to the seaboard. More or less tribute has been exacted by the rebel authorities on the creeks and rivers, the natural canals of China, and not a few have lost their lives. Besides, in many localities acres and acres of the mulberry, whose leaves feed the silk worm, have been devastated, as well as the tea. The amount of production has become less and less year after year; and thus, while the Chinese themselves have been great sufferers, the consumers of Europe and the United States also have been compelled to contribute indirectly to the caprice and wantonness of this fanaticism. What is still worse, is the fact that the Taepings do not succeed in retaining, even in their loyal districts, the respect of the people, and cannot rely upon the proper cultivation of the land. The farmer fears that he will be plundered of his rice and other produce, and is quite content to raise enough for his own immediate use, and stoically waits for peace. The native merchant is suspicious that he will be squeezed dry if he continues his business, so he is apt to hide his treasure and idle away his time in small gambling, or "lap himself in Elysium" in some opium-house. The rebel military chest, therefore, is usually replenished by some fresh foray into a district not before disturbed, and all classes are forcibly compelled to contribute their mite, and are glad to escape with their lives.

Such a state of things is unnatural in any country, and invariably comes to an end. It has culminated even here. This is not a fighting people. They prefer talk and trade to the knife and idleness. Labor and its necessity is the first lesson taught to the Chinese in infancy, and the conviction is produced that this is the way to propitiate the Evil Spirit — the only invisibility that the Chinese dread. According to their religious instruction, they have nothing to fear from the Good Spirit. But the Evil Spirit is in the wind, the water, the cloud, the raindrop, and in darkness and light, and must be propitiated.

As by the law of the land property descends to the eldest child — the male taking precedence of the female — and devise by legacy is not tolerated, large estates accumulate, and want and poverty abound. A large majority of the people are in the latter category, and their constant effort is to get the chow-chow of to-day. If successful in rising above the general mass, their every effort is to add to whatever is thus gained, even to the end of their lives.

The increase of property gives them no ambitious aspirations for political power. The Chinaman is content with being able to wear more and richer silks and satins, having at his elbow more and richer chow-chow, and enlarging his household. Indeed, they are slow to be ostentatious, though as vain as the peacock, lest the mandarin of their district should politely notice their improved condition, and some day without invitation request the favor of a cumshaw, or a trifling loan of a few thousand taels, of course never to be repaid.

It is this propensity to labor and trade which underlies and sustains the commerce of this big and populous empire. It was gigantic before the rebellion. It is large even now. The last census was taken some ten years ago, and the official records at Pekin foot up over 400,000,000 of souls. And why this record is not trustworthy, it is difficult to learn. It is worthy of belief, for it is compiled from the returns of the Tepaou in each census district, who is personally responsible for the land tax in his district, and which is assessed per capita upon the occupier of the land, who is liable to be dispossessed in case of non-payment. With such a vast population to work, feed and clothe, and blessed with fertile lands, rewarding the tiller of the soil with two and three crops every twelve months, no wonder that the people of the nations of the West and the Isles of the Seas are constantly seeking this far off country, and never fail to find a remunerating market.

CHAPTER XXI.

THE NEW TREATIES.

THE treaty of Wanghia provided that at the expiration of ten years, either party should have the right to propose additions and modifications. Experience demonstrated that, notwithstanding the trade had been extended tó new markets, still trade with the Empire at large remained unopened. Besides, a multitude of questions and disputes in the transaction of business, were daily occurring, and the necessity was more and more felt of having an opportunity of reaching more directly the ear of the Emperor. And hence that it was of great importance for the minister to have the right to go to Pekin, and there transact his official business on the footing of perfect equality. Accordingly, William B. Reed, a distinguished citizen of the state of Pennsylvania was appointed by the President of the United States minister to China, and directed to get a new treaty. This was accomplished in June 1858, and duly signed at Tientsin. By virtue of this new treaty two additional ports were opened to foreign trade, namely, Swatow, and Taiwan on the island of Formosa, and the tonnage duty was lessened one fifth. In November of the same year at Shanghai, the tariff of duties on imports and exports was materially modified and lessened, and provision made for the transportation and sale by the foreign merchant, inward and outward, to, from, and at any part of the interior, of merchandise and produce. For the first time in the history of treaty making with the government of China, this treaty of Tientsin provided that the missionary might pursue his calling at the ports opened to foreign trade, and receive the protection of government. It was likewise provided that all rights and privileges theretofore or thereafter granted to any other nation by the emperor, should at once enure to the United States. The English and French negotiated similar treaties the same year. The English treaty, in addition made provision for the opening of the ports of Tangchow, Tientsin, Newchwang, and three ports on the Yangtze river.

None of these new treaties, however, were to go into effect till they were duly ratified by the home government, and ratifications exchanged; and this was to transpire within one year thereafter.

CHAPTER XXII.

HOW THE NEW TREATIES WERE RATIFIED. — TAKU FORTS.

IN the following year, John E. Ward of Georgia, was appointed United States minister to China, and reached Shanghai in the month of May 1859. He had the ratified treaty, and was under instruction to proceed to Pekin and exchange ratifications. Mr. Bruce, the British minister, and M. Bourbillon the French minister, were also at Shanghai on a similar errand for their respective governments. These three envoys departed from Shanghai in June, intending to reach the seat of government by the way of Tientsin. When they arrived off the mouth of the Peiho river, they were informed by the Chinese governor general that it would be necessary for them to proceed nine miles further north, before they landed, where they would find conveyances to take them to Pekin, overland. They were also informed that the emperor was daily expecting their arrival and had made suitable arrangements for their accommodation whilst they sojourned at the capital. The British and French ministers declined to go farther north by water, and insisted that the new treaties conceded the right to go up the Peiho river. They were respectfully informed by the Chinese authorities that they were under orders without discretion to resist this, and if the ministers crossed the bar at the mouth of the river they would be exposed to the cannon of the Taku forts. These forts were built on opposite sides of the river a short distance above its mouth, near a town called Taku, and commanded the channel, which was narrow. They were constructed of mud and brick. After a careful examination, and believing that the resistance to their progress would be weak and soon overcome, the ministers of Great Britain and France crossed the bar with their fleet of gun boats, under the command of the British Admiral, Sir James Hope. As soon as the fleet got within range, the cannon of these mud forts opened upon it with deadly effect. Two vessels of the fleet were sunk, and the others were more or less battered and crippled. The cannonade was kept up for several hours, the fleet returning the fire briskly without producing a decisive result. Finally it was determined to land a party of marines and storm the forts. It was dark before a landing was effected, and the ground was found to be very soft. The force pushed forward over this esplanade as best they might, but were interrupted in their progress by a wide ditch, and the mud ankle deep, and sometimes going into it up to their knees. A portion of the party succeeded in reaching the walls, and attempted to scale them. But the fire of the Chinese was so heavy and destructive, and their resistance so stubborn, the order to retreat was given; and by the next day what remained of the fleet above water was retired in the offing. The British admiral was severely wounded. There were many casualties in the command, and the fleet in a few days returned to Shanghai.

In the mean time, the United States minister not finding any stipulation conceding the right to go to Pekin, either by the Peiho river or any other specific route, complied with the request of the Governor General, and traveled to Pekin overland. There he found commodious residences in readiness for the Treaty ministers, and learned to his satisfaction that the Imperial Government had not anticipated any hostile collision between the fleet and the Taku forts. He was the bearer of an autograph letter of credence from the President to the Emperor, and it was desirable to deliver the same in person. To this there was no objection, but the intimation was thrown out that he would be expected to *kotow* in the usual manner to the Emperor when ushered into his celestial presence. The United States Minister at once declared that he could not do this, and that he must meet the Emperor upon a footing of equality. He further declared that he was willing to comply with all the forms and ceremonies of that Court which were not derogatory to his government; but that he was there as the sole representative of the President, and he could tolerate no line of procedure that was inconsistent with perfect equality between the two governments.

From the backing and filling manifested on this point by the Emperor and his advisers, it was evident that he was quite desirous to have a personal interview with the American envoy. Perhaps this desire was superinduced by the affair at the Taku forts.—He, however, dared not depart from the usage of his predecessors so far as to dispense with the *kotow* altogether; and finally intimated that the slightest recognition of his celestial presence by the American Envoy would be deemed sufficient. The latter steadily declined to do any act that could be even perverted into a recognition of any attribute, terrestrial or celestial, which was not accorded to the President of the United States. It was arranged that the formal exchange of the ratification of the treaty should be made with the Governor General in his capacity as Minister for Foreign Affairs, and Mr. Ward returned to Shanghai in August.

Upon conference with the Minister for Foreign Affairs at Shanghai, Mr. Ward found there was a strong disinclination then to put the treaty into operation, and it soon transpired that this was owing to an anticipated rupture with England and France by reason of their repulse from before the Taku forts. Anxious to have citizens of the United States avail themselves of the two new ports of Swatow and Taiwan as well as the reduced tonnage duty as early as possible, Mr. Ward finally consented to postpone the execution of the treaty of Tientsin in every other respect until the English and French difficulties were settled. It was under this arrangement that the new American treaty went into effect.

It was now about time for the ministers of England and France, who were sojourning at Shanghai, to get replies from their respective governments indicative of their future line of policy with the Emperor. It was soon announced, that a large British and French force, naval and military, would appear in the Chinese waters the ensuing spring to demand indemnity for the past and security for the future; and that, during the interrim, their relations with the Imperial Government would continue upon the footing of their old treaties. After the lapse of a few weeks, their generals and other officers began to arrive by the mail route overland, the main body of their forces having been sent around by the Cape of Good Hope. It was late in the spring before these forces reached their destination. It was July before Lord Elgin, special Ambassador for England, and Baron Gros in the same capacity for France, had arrived out; and the allied forces again appeared off the Peiho in August 1860, though with more imposing and far greater strength than in the preceding year. They immediately commenced their work of reducing the forts. This work was finished in a few days, and then they started for Pekin. With the usual delays of skirmishing and negotiation at different points along the route, the allies finally sighted the walls of the imperial capital in October. The Emperor fled to Zehol in Tartary, the land of his ancestors. The allies burnt down one of his palaces called the "summer palace," some nine miles outside of the gates of the city, looted it of its well filled and very valuable treasures, embracing the richest of silks, satins, crapes, pearls, diamonds and precious stones, that had been accumulating there during a long series of years, and conquered a peace. They compelled the Imperial Government to agree to pay their war expenses; and as security it mortgaged in advance two fifths of the customs revenue from foreign trade; and thereupon their treaties made at Tientsin in June 1858, were proclaimed to be in full force and effect.

The additional advantage conferred upon foreign commerce by the British treaty, was the privilege of trading to the ports of Tangchow, Tientsin, and Newchwang in the north, and to the ports of Chin Kiang, Kew Kiang, and Han Kow on the great river Yangtze. The treaty likewise conceded to foreigners the right to travel in the interior upon the passport of the consul, countersigned by the intendant of circuit. It was provided however, that the bearer of the passport should not visit any place occupied by the Chinese rebels, on pain of forfeiting all protection, and liable to punishment by the authorities of his own country. These provisions virtually opened to the outside world a country of immense resources and wealth, which theretofore had been studiously locked up; and whose inhabitants by every preceding arrangement had been carefully and jealously withdrawn, as far as practicable, from mingling unrestrained with the people who came there from other lands. Trading on the great river commenced at once. Within the space of one year upward of twenty steam vessels were regularly and constantly employed in navigating it between Shanghai and Hankow, the upper port distant over eight hundred miles from the sea. The number of sailing craft in the interest of foreigners is over one hundred, and all doing a thriving business. They are laden upward for the most part with foreign merchandise and treasure, and return with valuable cargoes of tea and other native produce. The steamers carry passengers and the mails; and the Chinese avail themselves of this opportunity instead of jogging along in their native craft as in former days. This change is fast working a revolution in the old slow coach mode of transacting business with the Orientals, and the time probably is not far distant when foreign vessels will be as thick on the Yangtze as on the leading thoroughfares of Europe and America. Steam vessels, both side wheel and screw, are built in England and the United States, carried to China and there put together. The ship carpenter and the machinist of the West have already reached China. Hulls and machinery are now constructed there; and steamers of twenty-five tons carrying capacity and upwards, are launched for use on the Yangtze and smaller inland rivers and lakes. The Chinese are fast becoming the owners of these vessels. Ere the present generation shall have passed away, it is extremely probable that the antique junks and luggers, which have constituted the mercantile marine for thousands of years, at least in the vicinity of the great plain, will be supplanted by faster, larger, and less expensively navigated vessels of modern times.

CHAPTER XXIII.

SHANGHAI.

THE accommodations in the foreign settlements differ at the various ports. In most of the ports, the settlement is a mere huddle of houses and *godowns*, in the occupancy of foreigners. The one at Shanghai, however, rises to a higher grade. It is laid out like a city at home. It extends along the harbor for the distance of three miles, and has a breadth of one mile. It is laid out into wide and macadamized streets, well drained with brick sewers, has an abundance of public lamps to light the streets, an efficient and well organized police, a capacious race course, and neat and commodious buildings.

The residences of the merchants are large and elegantly finished, and admirably constructed for comfort. The rooms are high and airy, with windows opening to the surface of the floor upon a wide piazza, and thus affording proper ventilation for a hot and debilitating climate, and sufficient swing for the large *punkas* that fan them. Many of these residences cost twenty thousand taels to construct, and half as many for the furniture. They may be called, with propriety, palatial private hotels. One of them, it is said, cost the present proprietors one hundred thousand taels, equal to one hundred and forty-eight thousand dollars, United States currency. Another is reputed to be the most finished and best arranged establishment in every appointment in all the East Indies. It is proper to remark, that the proprietors of these luxurious and fascinating abodes hasten to open wide their doors to the wayfarer, and invariably greet him with a hearty welcome.

The settlement also has its church edifices, and Christian service is observed with as much regularity and punctuality as in Western lands. The buildings mostly are built of brick, and have large court yards, well supplied with plants and shrubbery.

The Press is also represented. There are two daily newspapers, and two weeklies, printed in the English language. The job printing is reputed to be lucrative. A perusal of the advertisements in the newspapers makes one feel at home.

Since the opening of the Yangtze river to foreign trade, the commerce of the port has greatly increased. It is the entrepot to Central China. The river is now navigable to Hankow, nearly one thousand miles inland, for sail and steam vessels, and enters the heart of China. The merchandise, both inward and outward, is unladen at Shanghai, and the duties are there paid. Sometimes the harbor is much crowded with foreign vessels, and a goodly number are always at anchor. Twenty nationalities are represented by as many consuls, vice consuls, and commercial agents. Five only, namely, the United States, British, French, Russian, and Prussian, are Treaty Powers, and their peoples enjoy the rights of exterritoriality. The Chinese countenance the others, and allow their peoples to trade the same as those of the Treaty Powers.

It is customary for each nationality to fly its flag daily, and the number is so many, that the Chinese frequently speak of the port as "a port of many flags."

The cost of living to the foreigner, is according to his taste for native or foreign eatables and drinkables. Europe and America send thither in excellent condition green vegetables, green corn, green peas, fresh butter, cheese, dried and smoked meats, preserved fruits and jams of every variety, wines also, and brandies. To these the foreigner quite naturally inclines; but as they are brought from afar, and many months must necessarily elapse before the shipper can get a return from his outlay, they command a high price for the consumer to pay.

Tropical fruits abound, and the market is supplied with game and an excellent quality of mutton. Irish potatoes are seldom seen. A palatable potato is raised in Macao and brought up the coast, but it is small, wet, and not very nutritious. Occasionally potatoes survive a voyage across the Pacific, from California, and are quickly caught up by the foreigners. The Chinese do not care for them, but a cargo of rice engages their attention as soon as it reaches port.

The native trade between this port and the interior, and up and down the coast, is large and profitable. The native craft, consisting of junks and small luggers for the creeks and rivers, at all times crowd the harbor. A portion of it is set apart for their exclusive use; and it is said that as many as ten thousand are often anchored at the same time. Their masts, when seen at a distance, present the appearance of a forest. They are similar to the North River sloops, and about the same burthen. The luggers are usually manned by a crew of ten, and the junks by twice that number.

It is a characteristic of the Chinese to go in crowds, whatever may be the work. And it is not exaggeration to say that one foreigner will do the work of three Chinese. The latter, however, work in patience in heat and cold, in rain and sunshine.

The native city is called Shanghai from its locality. The name is a compound of two Chinese characters translated *shang* and *hai*, and correspond in meaning with the English words *above* and *water*. The city is situate in latitude 31 deg. 12 min. north, and longitude 121 deg. 28 min. east from Greenwich, on the Wangpoo river, near its junction with the Soochoo creek, and twelve miles above the intersection of the Woosung river with the Yangtze, and fifty miles from the sea. The Wangpoo river and the Soochoo creek when united, form the Woosung. Vessels drawing twenty-two feet of water can cross the bar at the mouth of the Woosung, at spring tide, and come up to the harbor. The tides, however, are so strong, and the channel so tortuous at some points, that it is necessary to take a pilot.

The surrounding country is flat, and rice and cotton are the staple productions. There are no hills or mountains in sight, and it is necessary to travel many miles to reach them. The summer climate is hot and unhealthy, with little of rain or thunder and lightning. Weeks transpire without a drop or a roll or a flash. But when these elements do make their appearance, the whole heavens are vivid with the electric light, and the earth trembles with the reverberation of the terriffic peals of thunder, and the water pours from above in torrents. The Chinese consider the heavens as the residence of their celestial gods; and on these occasions they seem to believe that a fearful quarrel is raging among them on high. But, they say, a balance of power is preserved among these combatants for dominion in the sky; and when the sun — the lovely king of all — comes, the *melèe* subsides, and each again moves quietly on within his own peaceful orbit.

In the winter the climate is cold enough for a fire in the sitting room, and some ice is seen in the month of February. Snow is rare, though in the February of 1862, to the profound astonishment of all, it fell to the depth of two feet on the level. It soon disappeared however. The rays of the sun were too strong for it even at that season of the year. As the Chinese are superstitious, many were the predictions of good and evil on the happening of this event. Some went so far as to predict the downfall of the rebellion. Other wiseacres foretold the overthrow of the imperial government. All agreed that this big fall of snow was ominous of some extra event to come off during the current year. And when shortly after it was officially announced that the British and French forces were to be employed in aid of the Emperor, the vaticinations of the imperialists became prophecies fulfilled. The success thus far of the allies over the rebels strengthens these presentiments, and inclines the masses to have more confidence in the ability of their government to disperse treason, and restore order and tranquillity once more to their distracted country.

The foreign population of Shanghai permanently ashore is supposed to exceed two thousand. Add to this number eight thousand for those who belong to the shipping and for the troops, and we have in round numbers ten thousand as the quota of foreign population afloat and ashore at this port. Since Ningpo was seriously threatened by the rebels, the native population has largely increased. The merchants, gentry, and those of the lower classes who could get away, gradually and constantly left it for many weeks before it fell into the hands of the rebels, and when they finally got possession in December 1861, Ningpo may be said to have been depopulated. Most of these flying people in their hegira came to Shanghai. As Ningpo was a *Foo* city, it contained at least one million of souls. The native population of Shanghai is now estimated by the most careful calculators at one and a half millions.

Many of these Chinese are wealthy. It is often the case to meet with a Chinaman reputed to be worth one million of taels, and oftener of one hundred thousand taels, whilst one falls in with throngs who have their fifty thousand taels. In China error is not so apt to be committed in estimating a neighbor's property, as in the United States. For there is comparatively but little trust in commercial transactions. The balance due on the exchange of property is settled for the most part with silver, either in the shape of Mexican dollars, or sycee, that is, lumps of pure silver made in the shape of Chinese shoes, and therefore called shoes of sycee. It is customary to bury, or hide in some secure nook, these shoes till wanted. The Chinaman's property is in a tangible condition, and hence it is not difficult for him at all times to know the extent of it. His constant effort is to keep this knowledge away from the ears of the mandarins, so that he may escape being squeezed. At the same time, it is the constant effort of the mandarins to be well posted in this branch of knowledge. They squeeze often, and resort to various stratagems to gain their purpose.

CHAPTER XXIV.

SQUEEZERS.

IT is deemed a high honor to be the guest of the Toutai, that is, governor of a certain circuit of country. Once upon a time, as the story goes, the Toutai was unusually hard up for money. Though the customs furnished him with large amounts, and the various guilds, that is, associations of trades-people, had contributed liberally, yet the expense incurred in constantly fighting the *imps*, that is, the rebels, and of furnishing supplies to Pekin to enable the Emperor to repel the foreign devils, that is, the British and French, in their last war of 1860, had reduced his exchequer to a low point. He cast about in his mind where to replenish. He had found that sometimes the victim slipped through his fingers when he sent a subordinate mandarin to request the designed loan. The squeeze is always called a loan, though of course never to be repaid, and probably so understood by both parties, for a subject cannot sue a mandarin. So this time, as it was important to realize the money, the Toutai, as rumor hath it, invited a rich Chinese merchant to dine with him at his Yamun, that is, palace. The merchant felt himself extremely honored by this unexpected attention, and promptly accepted the invitation. He did not fail to be in attendance at the designated hour in full dress of silks, satin boots, and peacock feather, and was very politely received. He was served with a sumptuous banquet; and after a three hours' sitting, the servant brought in tea which, in Chinese etiquette, is a notice from the host to the guest that the entertainment is closed. The merchant soon indicated that he was about to retire highly delighted, when the Toutai quietly observed that his expenses were running high, and he was in a strait for sycee. The merchant did not take the Toutai's meaning and continued to bow himself out of the Toutai's presence. Whereupon the latter flatly added that he was under the necessity of requesting from him a loan of two hundred thousand taels!

"Hi yah!" exclaimed the astounded merchant as the truth flashed across his mind. "Impossible! Your excellency cannot mean what you say!"

"You have many holes of that amount of sycee,

and I ask you to empty only one," rejoined the placid Toutai.

The merchant hesitated to comply with the request, and stoutly insisted it was utterly impossible to get such a big heap of sycee. But the ice was broken, and the Toutai knew his man. So he quietly and pleasantly conducted the merchant to a cosy bed chamber near by, and politely invited him to enjoy it till his friends outside fetched to the Yamun the required sum. A fortnight after, one of his neighbors met the merchant on the street, and not having seen him for over a moon past, enquired if he had been to the tea and silk districts. The merchant said no, but he had been dining with the Toutai. The neighbor's envy was excited, but quickly subsided upon the merchant informing him that the dinner cost two hundred thousand taels.

The expenses of State during these rebel times run high; and the governors, whose duty it is to raise the means to defray them, are compelled to resort to many shifts. On another occasion, as dame rumor hath the story, the Toutai adopted the following method of discharging his duty to the emperor. The ammunition boxes were empty, and it was of the utmost moment that the same should be replenished forthwith. Now, trade in munitions of war is contraband, and especially so with the rebels. Still it is carried on constantly, and to such an extent, that one sometimes is led to think that the authorities wink at it. However that may be, on the occasion in question, the Toutai, or some person about his Yamun, it seems happened to know who dealt in the desired articles. A small button mandarin waited upon the dealer in contraband, and in a friendly way suggested that he had better see if he could not get a permit to land from a vessel then in port a large chop of powder and muskets. The dealer of course replied yes, and at once went to the Yamun. He got a permit, and before sundown the next day, the powder and muskets were snugly stowed ashore in his godown. Not far from the ensuing midnight, another small button mandarin called upon the dealer, and informed him that it was necessary to go to the Cheheen's office, that is, the district magistrate's office, to answer unto a charge of violating the revenue laws. The dealer briefly explained by what authority he had bought the powder and muskets, and vehemently protested against being so causelessly disturbed at such an unseasonable hour. The intrusive visitor then informed the dealer in contraband, it was for the purpose of enabling him to explain some previous transactions, that his attendance upon the Cheheen was now required. This was a new phase in this transaction, and the dealer's only alternative to save his head was to make terms without delay. He lost no time in making his wish to settle the matter known to the mandarin, who at once suggested that the dealer could not do better than to allow the coolies outside to take away the powder and muskets then in the godown, and perhaps that would end the affair. At any rate under such a disposition of it, the dealer need not then go to the Cheheen, as he would take the responsibility of so far obliging him at that late hour of the night, and would himself be responsible to the Cheheen for his appearance when called for. The dealer assented cheerfully, though his dealings under the permit were taking quite an unexpected turn, but fully resolved to keep clear thereafter from all dealings under permits. The ammunition boxes were thus amply replenished in good time; and the guardian of the province was in a situation to say to his superior that he did his duty, whenever called to an account for a lax administration of the revenue laws. It is a standing complaint that "the big fish eat up the little ones."

CHAPTER XXV.

CANTON.

CANTON, or *Quang Tung*, is in the south of China, in latitude 23 deg. 6 min. 9 sec. north, and longitude 113 deg. 15 min. east of Greenwich. It is situate on the north bank of the Pearl river, and not far from seventy miles above the sea. It is enclosed by a brick wall resting upon sandstone, is about six miles in circumference, and has twelve gates. It is divided into two divisions, called the old and new town. The high officials reside in the old town. The foreign settlement is near the southern part of the city, and consists of a few hongs and godowns.

This port was formerly the leading commercial emporium beyond the Cape of Good Hope. More foreign business was transacted here than at all the other open ports in China. Here were imported the drills, ginseng, and other merchandise for Central China. They were transported into the interior some two hundred miles, in boats, on creeks connecting with each other — then carried across a portage of forty miles on mules — and then reladen in boats, were taken to the many marts of trade in the centre and in the north-west of the Empire. The teas and silk and silk piece goods were transported in the same way and by the same route to Canton, and thence exported to Europe and America. Since the Yangtze river has been opened to foreign trade, all of these imports and exports have been diverted from their former route, and now ascend and descend the great river from and to Shanghai.

The native population is estimated at one million of souls. This estimate, probably, is not wide of the mark. The prevailing religion of this vast population is Buddhism. Buddha is their tutelary saint. But few are educated. They are very superstitious and irascible. Their propensity to pick a quarrel, and resent an injury and insult with the knife and bludgeon, far surpasses their race in all other parts of the Empire. They have more of the fighting character. They are the most reliable and best troops in the service of Taeping Wang, and wherever the rebels make their appearance, Cantonese are found among them. Most of the rebel generals hail from Canton.

The pirates who infest the bays and passes and inlets of the coast, are usually Cantonese. They are energetic and daring. They do not confine themselves to the native but also attack the foreign craft. A few months ago a party of them attacked with success an American steamer plying regularly on the Pearl river between Hong Kong, Macao and Canton. They took several lives, plundered the vessel, and then scuttled it. In order to have leisure to ransack the vessel free from molestation, they at first drove below the passengers and officers who did not escape by jumping overboard. This transaction was not occasioned by a sudden melée. The chief actors were on the steamer as passengers, and in pursuance of a premeditated plan to kill and rob. The captain and officers were foreigners. In other parts of the Empire, one foreigner on a native craft even, is quite sufficient protection against an attack from evil minded Chinese. It is not uncommon for the master of a junk or lugger to hire the service of a foreigner simply to ride on his vessel, because his mere presence will usually deter a piratical craft from coming along side. But the Cantonese are self-reliant, and appear to possess the courage of Western people.

The natives in the south of China are apt to waylay and attack foreigners. The boatmen who fetch and carry between the ships and the shore, are frequently reported at this nefarious business. They are reputed to be too apt to make way with a foreigner if the inducement is sufficient, when rowing or sculling him off to the ship after night-fall. Often bodies are seen floating in a decayed state about the harbor; and as sailors are transient persons, and rarely known outside of their little coterie, it is difficult to recognize these floating bodies. A Mexican dollar to an unprincipled boatman is a valuable acquisition, for it will furnish him with rice for twenty days — two thirds of a moon. Sailors, when they go ashore to kick up their heels in the dust, especially after long voyages — are apt to have many dollars in their fob. The long-haired Charon understands this perfectly well. He takes them ashore, a ready crony of the boatman greets jolly Jack at the landing, and straightway inveigles him to some drinking saloon hard by. Here the honest tar carouses till his dollars are gone, and then he is hustled aside for some fresh customer. If perchance the brain withstands the many and heavy draughts of beer and alcohol that Jack has taken aboard, and the idle wantons on either hand have not emptied his pockets, then comes the vocation of the nefarious and heartless boatman to finish the work which the saloon begun. And, if half what is told be true, unless the sailor keeps a good lookout ahead, he never reaches his bunk in the forecastle. To obviate such serious mishaps, it has become common for shipmasters to require their crews to go ashore in squads, so as to help each other in any extremity. But even then, they frequently go astray, and often under such circumstances never report for duty. A fruitless search leaves the master's mind in doubt whether the missing sailor has not deserted, and shipping another in his stead, the vessel raises anchor and goes to sea. If the missing man had a knife run into his vitals and was then pitched overboard, when afterwards his body rises to the surface of the water and is seen floating about the harbor, there is no person to recognize it, and all remembrance of it passeth away.

The Cantonese are skillful mechanics. They carve ivory, wood, stone, and brass; and their workmanship is exquisite. Living is cheap, and labor is cheap. Ten cents per day is more than the generality received for wages. The supply of labor exceeds the demand. The present generation have grown up since the foreign trade commenced. Those who frequent the open ports are familiar with foreign customs and manners, and the bars of separation are gradually being taken away. Business intercourse is more frequent and unrestrained. The natives have greater confidence in the good intention and integrity of the foreigners, especially those who belong to the treaty nations. A large number of the Cantonese emigrate to California. As many acquire wealth under the protection of the laws of the United States, a greater confidence in the goodness of that government prevails among the Chinese people. A constant trade is kept up between these people on both sides of the Pacific. It is a remunerative trade, or it would cease. The Chinaman's attachment to his native country is too strong and enduring to be consistent with his residence abroad, however temporary, if his pecuniary interest does not draw and hold him there. In either case, he desires his lifeless body to repose in the flowery land; and when one dies in another country, the surviving relative or friend makes every reasonable effort to take the body home to China. It is said, there is scarcely a ship sails from California bound to China, without having on board more or less of the Chinese dead.

CHAPTER XXVI.

HONG KONG.

HONG-KONG, or *Hiang Kiang*, is an island and formerly belonged to the Quang Tung province. It is now a British colony, having been ceded to the Queen first by the treaty of Canton in 1841, and secondly by the treaty of Nankin in 1842. It is situated off the east coast of China, in latitude 22 deg. 16 min. north, and longitude 114 deg. 14 min. east from Greenwich. It is about ten miles in length. Its breadth varies from seven miles to one mile, and is separated from the main land, by an estuary varying in width from one mile to one quarter of a mile. It is covered with high and precipitous mountains, rising from one to two thousand feet above the level of the sea. Scarcely any portion of it can be called a valley. The soil is barren. The Chinese, by close attention, succeed in raising a few vegetables. It is bare of forest, and there is a scanty undergrowth. Fish of excellent quantity abounds in the adjacent waters. On the island there are several Chinese settlements where the fishermen repair. There are supposed to be not far from one hundred thousand Chinese residing on the island, and two thousand foreigners. Victoria is the capital of the colony, and there the British authorities reside. The colony has a governor, legislative council and courts of judicature. The harbor is capacious and the anchorage is safe in deep water, close in shore. It is a call and see port, and the harbor is usually crowded with the shipping of every nation, and thousands of Chinese craft. It is a free port.

An extensive import trade is carried on in rice, sugar, alum, nut oil, dye stuffs, sulphur, and provisions of every sort. The exports are mainly manufactured goods, opium brought from India, and stones quarried on the Island. Many of the imports are exported, especially rice and sugar. Large quantities of the latter are sent to Australia and California. A large part of the vessels that reach Hong Kong depart without breaking bulk, or leaving a portion, proceed to the final port of discharge. The principal mercantile firms have houses at all of the open ports in China, and some of them also have agents in Japan. The house at Hong Kong determines from previous advices of the state of the market, where the vessel is to unload and load, unless otherwise ordered from home. Since the rebel raids over the tea and silk districts, it stands the merchant in hand to look sharp, so as to be well posted where the teas are to be taken on board. Indeed, this is probably the fact at all times, as prices and qualities vary at different ports. But the sly and shrewd Chinaman also has learned how to be posted in the markets of the Western world; and unless forced to sell — an unusual occurrence — clings stubbornly to his teas till a customer appears who is willing to pay the designated price. Then the teas are *settled*, that is, bought and paid for, *chop chop* that is, in a trice.

The inhabitants at Victoria have a hot climate. The high hills to the southward intercept the monsoon which prevails from the south-west during the summer months. To remedy this in some measure, as well as to get room for building purposes without being compelled always to blast the rocks and dig into the mountain, a small slice of ground on the main land opposite, known as Cowloon, was ceded to the Queen by the treaty of 1860, upon the adjustment of the terms of peace at the conclusion of her last war with the Emperor. This additional territory now belongs to the colony of Hong Kong, and affords eligible locations for amusements, and public and private residences.

In order to be turned to a good account for the avocations of commerce, it will be necessary to construct jetties extending out some distance from the beach, as the water is not deep close up on that side of the harbor. Victoria, however, probably will continue to hold the principal business, at least for many years. This capital has progressed too far with Western institutions not to remain the chief seat of the colony. It now has the court house, penitentiary, post office, and other public buildings, as well as churches, reading-rooms, libraries, and club-houses. Besides, the merchants have expended too many hundreds of thousands of dollars, in the construction of buildings and business conveniences of various kinds, to be inclined to abandon them in a hurry.

CHAPTER XXVII.

FOO-CHOO-FOO.— TEAS.— THE DIFFERENT KINDS.

FOO-CHOO-FOO is one of the open ports, and is situate in the province of Fo-kien, on the river Min, about twenty-five miles from its mouth. It is in latitude 26 deg. 12 min. 24 sec. north, and longitude 119 deg. 30 min. east from Greenwich. It is the capital of the province, is a *foo* city, and contains a population of over one million of souls. It is about seven miles in circumference, and is surrounded by a wall said to be thirty feet in height, and twelve feet in width at the base. It has large suburbs, and is surrounded by an amphitheatre of hills, from the summits of which, the sea can be descried in the distance. The anchorage for foreign vessels is in the river Min, and seven miles below the city. The water is too shallow for foreign vessels to approach nearer the city. Their cargoes, both inward and outward, are transported in lighters, that is, small covered boats which are sculled and rowed up and down this part of the river. It is necessary for vessels to take a pilot for the river navigation, as well as some distance out to sea. There are some islets off the mouth of the Min known as the "white dogs," and which are at the entrance to the pilotage ground. The most hazardous part of the river is near its mouth, as there is a dangerous rock in mid channel but far enough below the surface of the water to be invisible to the stranger. First and last, there have been several shipwrecks on this rock, and valuable cargoes lost.

The trade of this port is large. It extends up and down the coast. The communication with the Loo Choo islands and with Japan is of considerable importance. The principal exports are black teas, timber and fruits. The oranges are very desirable. The teas are brought from seventy to one hundred miles in the interior; and because they are usually of the black kind, an impression has been produced that black and green teas are not produced on the same bush or tree. It has been satisfactorily ascertained since the country has been opened to foreigners under the passport system, that the contrary is the fact. Both kinds are grown on the same tree. The difference in color as well as quality is to be attributed to the age of the leaf when picked, and the climate in which it is grown. The same tree in some latitudes and seasons has been known to produce leaves the decoction of which is both green and black, according to the season of the year that the leaves are gathered. But usually in the same latitude with a similarity of cold and heat, wet and dryness, the color of the decoction will be either green or black throughout the entire year. The quality of the tea is regulated by the age of the leaf when picked, as well as the manner in which it is dried and prepared for market. Young hyson is made from the young leaves picked in early spring. Old hyson, from the leaves of longer growth and greater exposure to the rays of the sun. The Chinese do not draw the tea over the fire when they wish to drink it, as is done in other countries. But they put the tea into the cup, pour in some hot water, put a lid over the cup, and then sip it off as their taste may dictate; of course not half of the virtue of the leaves is extracted; and it is said that the leaves are often gathered together, and months and years afterwards furnish delightful concoctions to the tea drinkers in other and distant portions of the globe.

The timber exported is pine in the log, from six to twenty-four inches in diameter. Large quantities of it are taken to Shanghai, and there used for building purposes. There are no saw-mills in China, as in the United States. Hence, the logs are sawed into boards and plank, by the hand saw. The imports are chiefly English and American drills, sugar, and salt. The latter article is manufactured in China to an extent sufficient in the main to supply the demand for home consumption. It is of good quality. The table salt has coarser grains than is agreeable to the taste of foreigners. It is a government monopoly.

The Governor General of the Province resides at Foo-choo-foo, and it is the chief city in Fo-Kien. It is usually written Foo-choo, the latter syllable *foo* being an addenda to designate the grade of the city. The climate is hot but not unhealthy. The streets are narrow and filthy, but several canals extend through the city, and afford an outlet for refuse and uncleanly water.

CHAPTER XXVIII.

AMOY.

AMOY, or *Heamun*, is another of the open ports, and is situated on an island of the same name in the Province of Fo-Kien. It is in latitude 24 deg. 10 min. 3 sec. north, and longitude 118 deg. 13 min. 5 sec. east of Greenwich. This city is at the southerly end of the island, near the mouth of two rivers that unite upon reaching the sea close by. One of these rivers passes by a large and populous city, not far distant in the interior, called Chang-choo-foo and of which Amoy is the sea port. The population of Amoy is represented to be nearly, if not quite, half a million of souls. The population of Amoy are mostly engaged in the coasting trade. They import cotton from India, foreign drills, iron, lead, steel, nuts, rice, and grain. They export teas, camphor, sugar, sugar candy, paper and earthen ware in large quantities. Sugar candy of the finest quality is brought from this port. The native merchants are reputed to be men of wealth and enterprise. The city is built on the slope of hills extending to the water's edge. The streets are narrow and dirty, from six to twelve feet wide, but the acclivity prevents the water from stagnating. Some of the streets are precipitous, and are ascended and descended by means of stone steps. Opposite the city towards the sea, is a small islet upon which most of the foreign community reside. It is fanned by the monsoon blowing from the sea, and though warm the climate is delightful, and probably the most healthy of all the ports opened to foreign trade. The anchorage for foreign ships lies between this islet and the city; it is easy of access, an abundance of water, a gentle tide, and room sufficient for the accommodation of a large fleet of vessels.

CHAPTER XXIX.

NINGPO.

NINGPO is still another of the open ports, and lies on a river of the same name twelve miles from its mouth, in lat. 29 deg. 51 min. north, lon. 121 deg. 32 min. east from Greenwich, in the province of Che Kiang. It is six miles in circumference, enclosed by walls twenty-five feet in height, and ten feet broad at the base. It has six gates. It is well supplied with shops and stores. There are large quantities of furniture made here, known as Ningpo furniture. The chief imports are drills, rice, provisions, fruits, spices, nuts, dye-woods, oil, and cotton; and its chief exports are tea, silk, furniture, wood and charcoal. The surrounding country, for several miles, is a valley covered with villages and hamlets. The people are industrious and thrifty, and some of the merchants are reputed to be possessed of very large wealth. There are many millionaires. Here also much attention is paid to education. There are several private schools. It is a *foo* city. It was conquered from the Emperor by the rebels, in the month of December 1861. The merchants and gentry took the alarm in season, and fled from their homes. Tens of thousands of the working classes also left the city. It is difficult therefore now to estimate the present population. There were probably one million of souls before the hegira. This event, of course, suspended the usual business of the port, and it is not easy to imagine when the same will be resumed.

CHAPTER XXX.

SWATOW AND TAIWAN. — TYPHOONS. — FORMOSA.

THESE two ports were opened to foreign trade under the American treaty of 1858. The former is situate in the province of Quang Tung, on the coast, about three hundred miles above Hong Kong, and contains a population of over one hundred thousand Chinese. A large foreign trade has sprung up there. The chief article of export is sugar, and of an excellent quality. The people are unruly and turbulent. It has long been known as the harbor of pirates.

It is visited every year with violent and destructive gales, called the typhoon, or big wind. Houses are blown down, and ships of the largest tonnage are swung from their moorings, and sometimes driven on shore, and there left high and dry. Such is the force of the wind, that the waves rise in a very few minutes to a great height — not unfrequently thirty and forty feet, and even higher. The barometer, and livid, leaden skies give timely notice, however, of the approach of these tornadoes, and the prudent and observant shipmaster prepares for them. They are ugly visitors, and universally dreaded. They usually occur in the months of August and October. Those of October are the most furious and destructive.

The anchorage for ships is several miles from the city, the water being too shallow to come close in. The country about Swatow is thickly populated, and fertile. The climate is hot, but is not regarded as insalubrious. The natives are hardy, and those of the city and near the sea, devote most of their time to fishing. They catch immense quantities of fine fish, and export much, dried and salted, to other ports. Opium was smuggled into this port for many years, and an illegitimate and lucrative trade carried on by small clipper vessels. This trade is now legalized, but it is doubtful whether it is as profitable as formerly, certainly not more so.

Tai-wan is a town of small note, and lies on the island of Formosa, near the southerly extremity, in latitude 23 deg. 8 min. north, and longitude 120 deg.

22 min. east from Greenwich. It is under the jurisdiction of the provincial authorities of the province of Fo Kien, and is nine miles from the main land. It is considered the principal town on the island. Many years ago the Dutch carried on a considerable trade there, and a large number of Chinese junks annually visited it. If tradition be true, it once had a fine harbor and easy of access. The entrance is now choked with accumulations of sand, and only vessels of light draught can now safely enter the harbor. Large vessels anchor outside, and the merchandise is now taken off and on by small boats.

The island of Formosa is reported to be two hundred and fifty miles in length from north to south, of an unequal breadth, with a maximum of one hundred miles, and divided by an uneven range of mountains, which rise at intervals to an extreme height. The elevation of the principal summits is estimated at ten thousand feet above the level of the sea, and covered with snow the year round. The whole island is claimed by the Emperor, and a quasi recognition of his rule prevails among the people. Along the Western coast of the island and for many miles inward, mandarins are to be found exercising their official functions in the many villages and hamlets. The people appear to acknowledge their supremacy. On the eastern slope of the island their fealty is looser and more indistinct. Indeed, the class of people who occupy the eastern side of the island may be called the aborigines; whilst the western side is filled with the descendants of Chinese who have emigrated to the island from time to time, during the last three centuries. The soil is fertile and climate salubrious. Large quantities of sugar cane, rice, maize, and wheat, are grown here, and the land abounds with oranges, melons, grapes, peaches, figs, apricots, pine apples, cocoa and areca nuts, pomegranates, and chestnuts. The latter are larger than those found in the United States, and not so relishable. They are mealy, but very nutritious. Salt is made here; and near a town called Kelung, towards the north end of the island, coal has been discovered. It is bituminous. The camphor tree flourishes here, and pine timber is found in various parts of the island.

Foreign vessels are constantly trading to Formosa. They frequent Kelung, and find a profitable traffic there, though not provided for by treaty stipulations. As many if not more, go to Kelung than to Taiwan. The people want green tea, and cotton goods, copper cash and sycee. In return, they offer the productions of the island. Camphor and camphor wood, and timber, and fruits, are exported, as well as rice, and maize. There have been some shipwrecks along the island, and the shipmasters complain of inattention and neglect on the part of the mandarins in affording proper protection and assistance. Even collusion with unprincipled salvors is alleged against the local Chinese authorities. Instances that have come to light lead to this conclusion. Of course, the way in which such transactions occur is so roundabout, that it is difficult to present the mandarin in bold relief, and expose his base complicity to the public gaze.

The native craft from all parts of China frequent the island. It is reported that as many as five hundred junks of the largest size annually come there, and drive a lucrative trade. As the islanders part with more merchandise than they take, it follows that large amounts of dollars and sycee are left behind in settlement of balances. The result is, that what the world in general calls wealth accumulates, and many of the inhabitants possess great estates. It is asserted, and probably it is a truth, that many of these estates belong to Chinese residing in the provinces who have leased land on the island from the emperor, and supply the laborers. In addition to reaping a rich harvest from these distant investments, the proprietor is the better enabled to keep his wealth a secret at his home, and thus escape a squeeze from the mandarin of his district. This view also accounts for the absence of those evidences of prosperity which wealth commonly indicates. For a country that is known to have been inhabited by a thrifty race during two hundred years, there are slender evidences of wealth and prosperity. No paved high roads, no stone bridges across the many creeks and rivers along which the springs and torrents of the mountains find their way to the sea, no lofty marble monuments — the tell-tales of a misty or glorious past — no storied pagodas, but few temples, and unattractive dwellings, characterize Formosa. If in the main, it has been a mere colony of enterprising speculators, as undoubtedly is the case, the enigma is solved, and its present appearance is satisfactorily accounted for. And this solution also brings to light another important fact, that people in the hoary east know the value of different climates, of distant possessions, of colonial commerce, and have brought this knowledge into practical requisition, in advance of the people of the Western nations.

CHAPTER XXXI.

CHIN-KIANG. — KIU-KIANG. — HANKOW.

THESE three cities were opened to foreign trade under the British treaty of 1858, but in consequence of the non-exchange of ratifications the same did not go into effect till the spring of 1861. They are situate on the Yangtze river, and are the only ports on that river where foreigners have the treaty right to dwell and do business.

Chin Kiang is near the imperial canal which reaches both sides of the river at this point, and is about two hundred miles by water above Shanghai. It was taken possession of by the rebels when they broke the lines of the imperial army around Nankin in the spring of 1860. The rebels sacked the city, and put many of the people to death. Previously there was considerable trade carried on there, and its nearness to the canal made it an important military point. Since the rebels ravaged it, there has been but little business transacted there. The entire country in its vicinity has also been overrun by these followers of Taeping Wang, and shared a similar fate. A custom house officer is stationed on an island near at hand in the river, and all vessels report to him as they pass up and down the river.

Kiu Kiang is some three hundred miles further up the river on the south bank, and is a town of note and importance. Its population is estimated to be over half a million. It is near the tea and silk districts which now have their outlet to foreign countries at this port. They are taken to Shanghai where the export duties are paid to the imperial government, and there are ladened on vessels that carry them to the marts on the other side of the globe. Kiu Kiang is an old city with narrow and dirty streets. It has many rich merchants and opulent gentry. It is surrounded by a fertile country, and has not yet suffered any serious injury from the civil war. The rebels have repeatedly endeavored to take it, but without success. The people are active and courageous; and the authorities, both civil and military, have been up to their duty. Cotton goods and sugar find a ready market there at reasonable prices. Rice, wheat, and beans, are raised in the surrounding country. Little if any is exported, as it is all needed for home consumption. The native craft that repair to this port reaches a large number, and it presents a scene of activity and business.

Hankow is at the head of legitimate navigation on the river. Under the Treaty, foreign merchant vessels have no right to proceed further up the river for the purpose of trade. It is about eight hundred miles from the sea, and is in the thirtieth degree of latitude north, and one hundred and fourteenth degree of longitude east from Greenwich. It is situate near the mouth of a river called Hang-yang, that empties into the Yangtze. Of itself the town is not very large, but near by are the large cities of Han-yang and Woo-chang. The latter is an extensive walled town, and is the capital of the province of Hoo-pe. These three towns are in sight of each other, with the river between them; and all constitute what is now considered as the port of Hankow. The population of the port of Hankow, embracing the three towns, is reckoned to exceed five millions of souls.

The native trade is very large, and this point is the great commercial centre of the north-western part of China. It is about six hundred miles inland from Canton, and a business communication has been kept up constantly for many ages, between these two commercial centres. The opening of the great river however, to foreign vessels, is fast changing their previous relative positions. Shanghai steps into the place of Canton in this respect, and now is fast becoming the entrepot of the merchandise that formerly entered and left central China at Canton.

With such a vast population as now dwells at Hankow, there must necessarily be a large consumption of production, no matter from what quarter it may come. The artisans, trades-people, and the common laborers, are almost innumerable. There is a numerous class of gentry who are reputed to be men of opulence, and gratify their taste for ease and luxurious living. The city of Woo-chang contains a great deal of riches. According to some accounts, the sums are fabulous. The lands of the adjacent country are fertile, and are industriously cultivated. About one hundred miles above Hankow are coal beds. The banks of the river are high, and in some places the coal is discernible in layers, from the edge of the water to the top of the bank. It is bituminous and of very good quality. Now that foreign enterprise is reaching this region of China, the probability is that these coal beds will feel the touch of

Western civilization. And it is quite necessary; for there are already so many steam vessels plying on the Yangtze, with the prospect of an immediate increase in the number, unless coals are supplied for their use nearer China, the cost of supplying the propelling power will far exceed the ordinary running expenses, and materially reduce the profits of business. As it is, most of the coals are brought from England and the United States, and command from sixteen to twenty dollars per ton. The coals which have been used from the beds of China give satisfaction. They are not as strong, and do not emit as much heat as American or English coals, and make more ashes. As labor is cheap, the beds can be worked at a much less cost in China than in England or the United States. The freight from the two last named countries will be saved, which now amounts to double the original cost of the article at home; and yet there are so many ways for its consumption, and the foreign coals are so well liked, — especially the American anthracite — that the market for foreign coals will probably continue good in the north of China for many years to come.

CHAPTER XXXII.

TANGCHOW.— CHE-FOO.— TIENTSIN. —THE EMPEROR.— NEW-CHWANG.

THESE three ports were opened to foreign trade under the British treaty of 1858. They are called the Northern ports.

Tangchow is a small town and of inconsiderable trade. The foreigners have not to any great extent, availed themselves of their treaty rights at this port. Instead, they have gone to a town of small note called Chee-foo, a port lying on a bay of the same name. It is in the province of Shan-tung, and some twenty miles from Tang-chow. The merchants have not deemed this port even of sufficient importance to establish trading houses there. The trade is small, and the ships do not approach within several miles of the landing place. The French landed a regiment of troops there at the termination of their last war with China; and these troops, together with one or more men-of war, have continued at the port and its vicinity. Several missionaries, American as well as British and French, have removed thither, and opened school houses, and made a beginning of missionary settlements in that region. In the summer of 1861, the rebels showed themselves in the Shang-tung provinces, in large force. They were marching upon Tang-chow and Chee-foo. The foreigners became alarmed for their own safety, for the rebels were plundering and killing the people in great numbers, as they progressed through the country. To stay their progress, if possible by Christian persuasion, two American missionaries — the Reverend Messrs. Parker and Holmes — went out to meet them, entirely unattended by guards, or other protection than such as their Heavenly Father vouchsafed. When thirty miles out from Chee-foo, these valiant warriors of Jesus of Bethlehem fell in with the vanguard of the rebels. Fluent in the language of the country, they managed to pass along unharmed, and soon reached the head quarters of the general. They entered his tent. They opened a conversation with him, in as calm and friendly tone and manner as the feelings of the hour would permit. They sought to persuade him not to advance farther towards the sea coast. He insisted upon subduing the people to the very edge of the water. They expostulated. He flew into a towering passion, and ordered his guards to behead these missionaries. This sudden and sanguinary mandate was instantly executed; and their poor bodies, lacerated in many parts, were cast out to rot unburied and unknown far, far away, from their native land. Missed by their families at the port, for too long an absence, though their errand into the country was well known, an outcry was raised, and the entire community, both native and foreign, was soon astir to get tidings of them. In the course of a few days, a mixed cavalcade of Chinese and foreigners reached the settlement, having in charge the remains of these two faithful deciples of the cross. They received a christian burial on this promontory of Shan-tung, and the ceaseless roll of the sea against its shaggy cliffs is their requiem. Chee-foo is about five hundred miles, by water, north of Shanghai. The land in its vicinity is productive. The large flat bean is raised in large quantities, and made into bean cake is exported to other provinces for manure and provender.

Tientsin takes a higher rank than Chee-foo among the open ports. It is situate in the province of

Pe-che-le, on the north bank of the Peiho river thirty miles by the winding of the river, from its mouth, but not over twenty miles in a straight line. It is the head of navigation on the river for vessels from sea, and it is the seaport of Pekin. In consequence it is regarded as an important place by the Chinese, and is widely known throughout the empire. It is seventy miles in a south-easternly direction from the imperial capital, and is the entrepot of salt for northern China. Small boats ply on the creeks that intersect each other between it and Pekin. The latter place is supplied with rice from the south through this port. The town is pleasantly located upon the river, has many fine Chinese temples and other public buildings, and its population is said to exceed one hundred thousand. It has many wealthy inhabitants. Several are estimated to be worth rising of one million of taels. The people throughout the province are in the main said to be forehanded. It is believed that the wealthiest man in all China resides in this province. His riches are calculated at over thirty five-millions of taels. The estates of many others are put at three, four, and five millions. As by law the property of the parents descends to the eldest male child, and in default of issue to the nearest kin, it is not incredible that big estates should accumulate through a long line of provident ancestry.

On account of its contiguity to the seat of the general government, the people of Tientsin speak the court language — called Mandarin — more than is usual among the common classes in other provinces. They are a quiet, loyal, and money-making people. The climate is healthy. The weather is cold in the winter months, as it is as far north as the thirty-ninth degree of north latitude. In the summer months there is much heat, and the thermometer rises sometimes to the ninety-sixth degree of Fahrenheit. The people are fond of traffic, and are reputed to be faithful to their engagements. They import large quantities of grain, woolens and furs. Opium also finds a ready market here, and several hundred chests are annually disposed of at remunerative prices. The river is easily navigated by sailing vessels of light draught, the channel across the bar at the mouth being the most difficult and dangerous. Small sized steam craft also go up and down without difficulty. The only drawback to trade at this port is "the freezing up" in winter. The river is covered with solid ice as early as December, and is not free from it till March. This is an interruption to commercial pursuits seaward, that does not occur at the southern ports. Snow falls soon after the ice makes, and often to the depth of four or five feet.

Tientsin, so far as the foreign trade is concerned, is regarded as the most important of the northern ports. Through it, the merchants reach the fertile lands and inviting commerce of northern China. Previous to the negotiation of the last treaties, this part of the empire was wholly inaccessible to the people of other nations, unless they perchance wandered there in contravention of public engagements. Now they can penetrate into the interior, mingle freely with the Chinese, and sell and buy merchandise face to face without the entanglement of dilatory and circumlocutory middle men. The trade will enhance under such auspices; and apace, as it enhances, with proper prudence will grow the desire of the native dealer to come in closer contact with the foreigner in all the manifold transactions of commerce. And what is of greater moment, so far as the opening of this port is concerned, is its nearness to Pekin. Facilities are provided for the just and speedy settlement of all vexatious disputes that unavoidably arise from time to time, in the multiplicity of active commercial pursuits. A more equal and humane temper will thus be created and preserved between the several nationalities, and lead to wider and more inexhaustible fields of commercial enterprise and prosperity

The Peiho river has become world renowned. The military events that have occurred upon its banks make it classic ground. It was the mud forts at Taku which called forth the demonstrations of the British admiral in June 1858. The same fortifications repaired and more strongly manned, again summoned the united powers of Great Britain and France, in June 1859. In August 1860, they again gallantly replied to the thundering and damaging salutations of the allied forces both by land and sea. Twice had they virtually triumphed over their valiant and unsatisfied assailants. Once by the wily and easy diplomacy of asking nothing and promishing every thing asked for, and once by positive and inexorable force. Now, the celestial Emperor had called from Tartary his best lancers and most trusty warriors. He had gathered from far and near, a mighty host, and it moved to the deadly conflict under a forest of banners. The faithful matchlock and the potent gingall were in active requisition, and thousands of fighting men laid down their lives. But all to no purpose. The forts could not withstand the shock, and tear, and carnage, of the grape, and canister, and iron balls, which the allied batteries for hours incessantly poured into them. They surrendered; and diplomacy commenced at the point where powder left off. Cessation of open hostilities ensued for a brief season, during which time the land forces of the allies advanced up the Peiho to Tientsin. Simultaneously, the imperial legions retired still farther beyond, and massed themselves for another bout midway to the Celestial city. They were under the lead of Sang-ko-lin-sem, and the Prince of I. When the imperial army was in readiness to receive again the fire of the enemy, the negotiations of peace ceased, and the chariot wheels of war were again put in motion. This time they did not stop till the summer palace of his imperial majesty had been thoroughly sacked, and every track and trace of it had perished in flame. Then diplomacy resumed its wonted task, the terms of pacification were settled and sealed, and peace inaugurated. In the mean time, the Emperor had taken the alarm for his personal safety, and escaped to his beloved Zehol in the impregnable wilds of Tartary. Prince Kung was his representative at the capital, amicably and satisfactorily arranged the demands of the enemy and met the British and French ambassadors in the great hall of reception. His subsequent administration of national affairs evinces his inflexible determination to stand fast to the treaty stipulations, and carry them out in good faith. The absconding Emperor never returned to Pekin — he sickened and wasted away under his excessive debauchery, and finally died at Zehol in August 1861, in the thirtieth year of his age. He left a son in his twelfth year, who assumed the sovereign power immediately upon the decease of his father. The young Emperor has the advice of a counsel of regency till he attains his majority. His mother however, guides in fact the vermillion pencil. She is a woman of masculine will, and evidences great knowledge and tact in the administration of public affairs. A portion of the high officers of state at the decease of the late Emperor were opposed to the new treaties; and, as opportunity offered, threw stumbling blocks in the way of those of the high officers, who were endeavoring to comply with the new stipulations. Prince Kung withstood this opposition as long as his patience would enable him to do so, and when this ceased to be a virtue he quietly repaired to Zehol, where the young Emperor and his august mother were sojourning. He represented the situation of the Imperial court to the Emperor, and returned to Pekin. He carried back a decree which called for the instant death of the refractory ministers. He had no sooner reached the capital than each of these ministers without the knowledge of the other, at the hour of midnight, were arrested. The decree was executed to the profound astonishment of the residue of the imperial court.

New-chwang lies in a north-easterly direction from Teintsin, and distant therefrom about three hundred miles. It is in the most northern province. The town is situate upon a river some twenty-five miles from the sea, and is reputed to have a population of over one hundred thousand. The country in that region of China is productive. Wheat, maize, and beans, are raised in sufficient quantities to supply the home demand. Apples and pears are grown there similar to those in the United States, but not of as good quality. The apples rot very quick after they are gathered in the autumn. The pears are hard and unpalatable to an American, who has been accustomed to eat a fruit of that name in his own country. The Chinese, however, eat them with great gusto, uncooked and baked. They raise more than enough for their own supply, and send thousands of piculs to the more southern ports. The climate is cold. The winter weather is severe. They have heavy snow storms with violent winds, and the snow sometimes falls to a great depth. These storms extend far out to sea, and render the navigation of these waters in winter difficult and hazardous. An American ship was wrecked in the winter of 1862 near the entrance to the river, and became a total loss. The weather was too hazy to see how to steer the ship, and it took the ground. Unable to get timely assistance, the vessel broke up and went to pieces.

The people are stout, hardy, and courageous. Their demeanor towards foreigners is of a more independent cast than is usual at the other open ports. This may be accounted for upon the hypothesis, that their locality has not yet been the theatre of foreign hostilities; and they have not yet lived sufficiently long, side by side with foreigners, to appreciate the inequality of the two races. They act as if they had a country and government of their own, and were actually at home. They have not yet come to regard the foreigner as a permanent settler, or the foreign trade as a permanent institution in their kingdom. But they consider him and it as merely temporary, and suppose that people come to that country from afar because it is a better country. It is a common occurrence for them to inquire, why people leave their own country and travel so far, if it is equally good. When they shall have learned the value of an extended commerce, and the benefits that nations derive from the interchange of their productions, they will cease to put the question. As it is, the traders of New-chwang are too haughty and reserved in their dealings with foreigners. Self-interest will probably soon overcome this, and the gunboats and frigates will show them their littleness and inequality when weighed in the scale of civilized nations.

Traveling in the interior near New-chwang, and between there and Tientsin overland, is not deemed very safe. The roads are infested with highway robbers. They do not appear to know, or if they do know to care, about the treaty stipulations. Like the bandits of other countries, they enforce the injunction of "stand and deliver," and recognize no passport system that over-rides this favorite law of the road. Their organizations are said to be too strong for the Mandarins to suppress. They have existed from time immemorial, and overmatch all the efforts of the government to put an end to their calling. The natives are loud in their complaints against this illegal tyranny, and in consequence go in squads when they travel through the country.

It has been surmised, and the surmise has ripened into belief in some quarters, that the mandarins, like officials in some other countries, are in complicity with these highway extortioners and plunderers. If such is the fact, it is simply another mode of carrying out their system of "squeezing" from the loyal subjects, the gains of an honest and thrifty livelihood.

Wood, woolens and furs are scarce, and needed in this cold climate. To make the fuel go as far as possible, it is customary to construct wide and flat brick ovens six to eight feet in length for cooking and other purposes, and in cold weather spread out the bedding upon the top, and sleep there. The warmth of the oven makes a warm and comfortable couch. It is not uncommon for a dozen persons to occupy the top of the oven at the same time — men women and children. The farmers raise sheep, and frequently have large flocks. The wool is long and coarse. It makes warm clothing. The skin is usually cured with the wool on, and in that condition made into a garment, and used by all classes in the extreme cold weather. The mutton is better than is produced in England, Spain, or Saxony. It is tender, juicy, and fat; and there is no taste or smell of the sheep, when cooked and served upon the table. The gentry, merchants, and farmers, are good livers; and the same observation applies with equal truth, to most of all the other classes of this community.

The currency before the port was opened, consisted mostly of the copper cash cóined at the imperial mints. Their commercial dealings brought them but little silver. Much of their trade was with the Russians from the Amoor river and Siberia. Furs and tallow were the principal articles which they got in exchange for their commodities. Rarely did they get sycee from any quarter. And when they did get any, it generally came from their own countrymen at the south. Since the port was opened to the foreign trade, barter takes a different direction, and is of a different character. Now, these northern traders get dollars in settlement of balances, as well as the much coveted lumps of sycee. One satisfactory transaction of barter with the foreigner, stimulates them to engage in transactions of bigger magnitude; and thus their hitherto unknown commerce goes forth to mingle with that of other countries, in the emporiums of the globe.

CHAPTER XXXIII.

THE COAST.—PIRATES.—CHUSAN.

THE coast of China is better known than the interior. It extends through thirty degrees of latitude. It is of irregular outline, bold and rocky. There are not many large gulfs, or long arms of the sea. The gulf of Pee-chee-lee, into which the Peiho river empties, is the largest. From the southern line to the neighborhood of Canton, the coast lies low, and is approached from the interior over gravelly and sandy flats. In some places near the mouths of creeks and rivers, the soil is alluvial. From Canton to the Yangtze river, it is full of indentations, and lined with large and small islands. Among these many islands there are numerous bays and coves. They afford shelter to the thousands of small vessels that are constantly afloat. The fishing smacks are really innumerable. All the way from Hong Kong to Shanghai, the eye never fails to catch a glimpse of some of them. Many a wayfarer has counted a thousand in sight, day after day. They are usually manned with eight to ten persons, and often more. Whilst a portion are managing the little vessels, others are trolling the line, and throwing, and watching, and drawing in the net. The hauls of fish are often by the bushels. They catch perch, pickerel, bass, shad, eels, and a fish called pike in some parts of the United States. At the north in the vicinity of New-chwang, there is much successful fishing for cod and salmon. The fish are salted, or dried and smoked, when got ashore, and sent off to the large inland cities, where they find a never failing market. This business is the occupation of tens of thousands of Chinese.

From the Yangtze to the bay of Chee-foo, the coast is approached from the high hills and mountains far back in the country, by gentle declivities. The beach is sandy, and the tide at many points sweeps over very wide swales. Oftentimes, vessels venturing too near in shore are left by the ebbing waters aground on these ugly swales, miles away from the deep sea. The only chance of escape from destruction, is to keep a good watch on the lookout for the land and water thieves who are apt to infest these swales, and await the returning tide. From Chee-foo northward, the outline is more undulating with rock and swale.

Many stories are recounted of personal adventure along these coasts. There is scarcely an islet or a headland, that tradition does not connect with some wonderful event. They have been traversed for centuries by daring and reckless spirits. The peaceable merchantman has always essayed to reach the laudable profits of the carrying trade, and the shrewd dealers in merchandise have vied with each other to share, if not to monopolize the business.

Lawless rovers of the sea have made the navigation very hazardous, from the time when the memory of man runneth not to the contrary, and continue their piratical work to the present day. No year passes without chronicling the destruction of many junks, and the seizure of many valuable cargoes. If perchance men of fortune or position are found upon the vessel, their friends in some circuitous way are advised where they can be seen, and they are held in close confinement till the designated ransom is paid. To add to this enormity, the pirates name the time when the grace of ransom will terminate. It often happens that the sum is too high for the friends of the prisoner to raise, and he forfeits his head. Oftentimes the pirates condescend to release the cargo upon being paid a satisfactory amount of money in commutation. This line of conduct shows the weakness of the government in affording proper protection to the people. Indeed, it is so peculiar and different from every other government that is supplied with a moiety of as much machinery of state to enforce obedience to law, that, many are so uncharitable as to charge the mandarins to be in collusion with the pirates. It is uncommon, however, to molest foreign vessels, though not because they are foreign, but from the pirate's fear of being overcome. The coves and bays among the numerous groups of islands, afford eligible harbors of refuge for the outlaws, and make it difficult for the war junks and gun boats that go in search to find them. They are too apt to escape the vigilance of this police of the sea and thus ply their vocation with impunity. Their usual haunts, however, are now becoming so well known, that they do not of late get off so easily. Several of their nests, under the shade of projecting cliffs and tortuous estuaries that meander among the numerous islets, are broken up, many have been recaptured, and themselves brought to punishment.

It has been estimated by Chinese speculators upon this subject, that the value of these depredations, on an average from year to year, exceed five millions of taels,— an enormous tribute to be levied upon a legitimate and peaceful commerce!

It is delightful for the traveler to pass along the sea coast, when in a vessel that is deemed safe from piratical intrusion. The dash and wash of the water has made all sorts of images out of the rocks; and carved and smoothed them with all the artistical skill of the sculptor. The broad and high hills often rise to the elevation of mountains, and generally are tillable to their very summits. Mounds that enclose the remains of patriarchs and their descendants of ancient times, and monuments of marble in the forms of beasts and birds in memory of some distinguished man or event of centuries ago, relieve the monotony of luxuriant fields and barren headlands. Perhaps there may not be seen anywhere in the wide world, more beautiful or inspiring scenery than in the Chusan archipelago. This sea of isles is off the coast of Che-kiang, between Ningpo and Shanghai.

The archipelago may be considered about twelve miles in length from west to east. It has not a uniformity of breadth from north to south. It ranges from six to thirty miles. The line of circumference probably, would reach over one hundred miles. The principal of these islands is called Chusan, and from it the whole group takes the name by which they are generally known. They are interspersed with lofty hills that rise to a great height, and some to the height of one thousand feet above the level of the sea. There are many that ascend six hundred feet. Beautiful and fertile valleys nestle at their base, and are thickly populated. The sides of the hills are under close cultivation. Rice is often planted on artificial terraces rising one above the other, across the declivities. The water-courses from above are diverted into those terraces, sufficient moisture is thus obtained for the nourishment of the plant, and large crops reward the toil of the farmer. There is a town of considerable size, situate at the southern extremity of Chusan, called Ting-hai. This is the mart of the people on that island, and is under the immediate rule of a small button mandarin. The general reputation of this island, however, is not enviable, as it has attained the notoriety of harboring pirates; and is known and spoken of in that connection far and near. It is also regarded as the stopping place of smugglers and runaways from justice. It has been said that many of the native vessels which trade from Ningpo to Shanghai, pay tribute to these mercenaries to be allowed to navigate the archipelago in peace. However it may be, there are others who do not succumb to such a species of piracy; and the result is that they are molested when a favorable opportunity offers, and the marauders are occasionally caught and get their just deserts.

CHAPTER XXXIV.

PUNISHMENTS.— YEH.— HO.

THE criminal jurisprudence of China differs from other countries of modern organization. Punishment is inflicted to prevent crime, it is true, but the mode of infliction is widely different from that in vogue in Christian states. It is divided into three classes, namely, death, chastisement, and restraint of personal liberty. The punishment of death consists of beheading and disembowelment. The first is dealt in this manner. The victim is led to the field of blood, thrown lengthwise upon the ground, lying upon his back with the face uppermost, the feet are tied together and the hands the same, two policemen stand at either extremity of the victim, whilst the chief executioner chops off the head with a broad and thin bladed axe. The blow descends upon the throat, and rarely does one blow effect the purpose.

More frequently it is repeated several times before the head is wholly severed from the trunk. The head is then exposed to the view of the public, for several days, from the walls of the city. Sometimes, it is exposed to the public on bridges, especially those that span much frequented thoroughfares. Disembowelment is performed in this wise. The victim is led to the usual field of execution, denuded, stretched upon the ground with the face uppermost, hands and feet bound tightly together, two policemen at either extremity. The chief executioner is supplied with a straight sharp knife, well whetted for the occasion. With this instrument he makes a deep incision into the front of the body, from the neck to the abdomen. Then with the naked hand he tears out the heart, which, like the head in the former case, is exposed to the view of the public. If the executioner goes beyond this, and commits those acts of barbarity that are occasionly depicted by some bystander, he exceeds his duty, and is liable to punishment; and if he was in a country where strict official accountability is enforced, he would be summoned to his reckoning. The word disembowelment as used in the English sense, does not express the true meaning of the Chinese in this connection. They consider the heart the seat of all the virtues and vices of good and evil, and the life of the soul. With the decease of the body, they believe the soul transmigrates if left undisturbed; and when the heart is violently thrust out of the body, the purpose is to annihilate the soul for all time to come, and forever withdraw from it the elysium of immortality.

Whoever designedly sheds another's blood, incurs the death penalty, and whether disembowelment shall be added depends upon the atrocity of the crime. Whoever violently breaks into another's compound, and steals therefrom, incurs the death penalty, and whoever plots against the life of the State must forfeit his life.

Chastisement is inflicted for disobedience of law. According to Chinese theory, the Emperor is to rule and govern, as a father would rule and govern his family. It is his right and duty to visit his people with stripes, as his will may dictate; and this mode of punishment is resorted to daily in the courts of the land. It usually consists of ten to thirty blows with a small stick of bamboo. These blows are inflicted upon the palms of the hands, the soles of the feet, and the naked back, indiscriminately, according to the caprice of the magistrate. If a Chinaman is charged with any delinquency, and when arraigned to answer for it denies it, he is usually visited with stripes. If he is obdurate, he is remanded to his place of confinement. After a short interval of time has elapsed, he is again led into court. If he still persists in his innocence, he is re-visited with stripes. By and by, the magistrate again calls for him. If he still pleads not guilty, and cannot prove his innocence, and has not rich friends at his elbow, he is again flogged and remanded to prison. Some instances are known, of persons thus whipped and re-whipped, remaining in confinement till they die. If they convince the magistrate of their innocence, then the complainant is flogged instead, unless he buys himself off. If the delinquency is admitted, the prisoner receives the stripes and goes his way. Flogging is administered for such offences as in Christian countries would be visited with fine, or a few days imprisonment in some house of correction. If one owes a debt and does not pay it at maturity, or when called upon after maturity, instead of being sent to jail as in some countries, and there kept till the debtor pays the debt or " swears out," the Chinese debtor is flogged and admonished to keep his word in the future.

Imprisonment as a punishment is not practised in China. There are no sentences for a specific time of confinement. Restraint of personal liberty in most instances is merely used as auxiliary to the discovery of truth. There are no penitentiaries for the punishment of offenders, as in Christain communities. The prison houses for the confinement of persons charged with the commission of offences are loosely constructed, and too weak to resist the machinations of expert rogues. They are kept in a slovenly condition — too much so for a foreigner to remain in them for any great length of time and retain health, or even life. To guard against the escape of prisoners, they are securely bound, and at all times are under the close surveillance of a guard. It is a rare occurrence for an inmate to escape from his confinement, or to elude the vigilance of his keeper. Horrid accounts are given of transactions that sometimes occur within the gates. They appear to be too incredible for belief. The foreigners of treaty nations are exempt from being cast into them. The rights of exterritoriality removes them from the jurisdiction of the Chinese authorities. They are subordinate only to their own.

Chinese convicted of kidnapping, of violating the

police regulations, or of committing some wanton act of trespass, are oftentimes sentenced to stand or sit or lie in the same posture for a given period of time. They are sometimes put into the stocks, or carried about in cages, or fastened into a machine called the Cangue — an instrument of punishment peculiar to China. When used, it is in an upright position. There are holes for the legs and head of the victim, who is required to occupy it a given number of hours for a given number of days, in some public place, and often exposed to the rays of a hot sun, and the jeers of the populace who pass by. This confinement occasions severe pain. It is said that deaths have occurred in the Cangue, from sheer exhaustion. The duration of each day's confinement usually extends through six hours. When it takes place in the summer months, the wonder is that all its sufferers do not die. The Chinese are distinguished for their stoicism, but in no instances do they exhibit this peculiar trait of character to a greater extent than when undergoing the pains of the Cangue. If a single sitting terminated the punishment, one might imagine how the convict could muster enough fortitude to appear to treat it with apathy. But, the repetition day after day for one or more months without eliciting a single sigh or painful emotion from the sufferer, exhibits a power of self-control difficult to comprehend, and more difficult to credit if it had not been often seen.

Perhaps, this trait attains an equal degree of amazement in cases of suicide. Especially, when the Board of Censors at Pekin complains to the Emperor of the official delinquency of some big button mandarin. In such cases the mandarin receives from the Emperor an order, signed with the vermillion pencil, to repair to his presence. If upon examination the delinquency is not satisfactorily explained, the penalty being death, the Emperor allows the mandarin " benefit of clergy," by intimating to him the necessity of repairing to the temple. This intimation of itself advises the culprit of the adverse decision of the Emperor, and that he must lose his head. Now if his head is cut off by the public executioner, his property is confiscated to the State, and his blood is attainted even to the third and fourth generations. To prevent this, he cuts off his own head, or in other words takes his own life, without delay.

The mandarin does not exhibit the same alacrity in complying with the summons to come to the Emperor, unless he is well satisfied that he shall return from the ordeal unhurt. On the contrary, he avails himself of every procrastination, in the meantime bringing into his interest at the foot of the throne, all the back stairs influence that his official position and pecuniary resources can reach. It is said that Yeh, the former Governor General and commissioner for foreign affairs at Canton, on more than one occasion was the recipient of this famous order, and as often exhibited his official robes free from every stain in the eyes of his august master. It was not his destiny to commit suicide in the imperial capital. It was his lot to die on the banks of the far off Ganges, away from his kindred and native land.

Ho, his successor to the foreign portfolio, and the Governor General of the two Kiangs, did not fare so well. Ho resided at the city of Chang-chow in the neighborhood of Nankin. When the rebels, in the spring of 1360, broke the Imperial lines around the latter city, and overrun the country, taking Chang-chow and the rich city of Soo-choo, Ho became desperate, and abandoning place after place, finally brought up at Shanghai. When this appalling disaster became known to the Emperor, Ho was immediately sent for. The order found him delightfully inebriated with opium. He had taken his quarters on a mandarin boat in the harbor. and was surrounded with his attendants. He continued in this blissful state, with only short intervals, for several weeks. Ho was very rich. Finally his old father came to see him. The Emperor was solicitous to know why the Governor General did not make his appearance. Word was sent that he was sick unto death, and therefore unable to undertake so long a journey. Time was asked for and granted. Ho, under the direction of his father, did not get well, but continued sick month after month, till the time reached unto a year and more. Ho had an assistant in his foreign bureau by the name of Seih. This last named mandarin was very rich, but had large political ambition. Ho was deposed from office, and Seih installed in his stead, Ho prefering disgrace to death. This arrangement eased the mind of the Emperor, and was a most satisfactory arrangement to the Chinese authorities at Shanghai. Ho had saved and bagged all his riches, was occupying his marine quarters in quiet, and soon became not so sick but that he could attend the luxurious banquets of the Toutai and the new imperial commissioner for foreign affairs. His fortunes had taken a felicitous turn, and he was once more on happy terms with his evil spirit.

One day intelligence reached the port, that Lan— who had been deposed from the position of Toutai by the interposition of Ho in former years, and whom Seih succeeded,— had reached Pekin after a long journey, and having been suddenly attacked with a cough had died; in other words, committed suicide. This created a fluttering among the retainers of Ho and Sieh, which had not subsided, when two or three days afterwards the Emperor's decree reached Shanghai ordering a thorough search for Ho, and his arrest, and if arrested, directing him to be brought to Pekin without further delay. Of course the magistrate issued the usual warrant for his immediate arrest. What came of it did not transpire. His marine quarters were changed, and rumor had it in a few days that Ho was dead, having fallen in a fit of apoplexy. Truly Chinese punishments are sanguinary. Christian enlightenment only can ameliorate them.

CHAPTER XXXV.

RELIGION.

BUDDHISM is the prevailing religion among the Chinese. Buddha is the great god before all other gods. They have a priesthood who administer at the temples, attend funerals, witness marriages, and are present at many meetings on holidays. Their heads are closely shaved, as well as their faces. They do not wear the tail like the other classes of their countrymen, and wear no head dress or covering. They wear loosely a light colored gown extending to the ankles, and plain shoes. They do not receive stipends, but subsist upon alms and the small perquisites thrown in their way by worshippers at the temples. Usually they embrace the calling at an early age, and are taught by their seniors the precepts of Confucius, and the practical duties of their order of priesthood. Tanism, that is demon worship, once was prevalent among the Mongolians, but it does not now appear to be recognized. The sacerdotal college at Pekin regulates the priesthood throughout the empire. Their rituals and tenets are the same. The number is unlimited. They live a secluded life. They do not have libraries or many books. They do not write essays or sermons, and appear to be lazy and unambitious. They live in the temples, commonly called joss houses, after the idol or image which is given that name by the people. The temples in the country are often erected at the foot of some hill, or in the gorge of some mountain. Out of the way localities are the most favorite spots for the ceremonies of the temples, and the abodes of their ministers, who lead a life of celibacy. There is a small island among the Chusan group, which is wholly occupied by the priests, and thither the votaries of Buddha repair from far and near, to gain the favor of their Gods. It is said that the pirates make an annual visit to this island, and leave large sums of money at the temples to gain absolution for their many offences. The island is interspersed with hill and dale, woodlands and improved fields, and presents a picturesque and inviting aspect. On one side of the island there is a precipice two hundred feet in height reaching to the sea that washes its rocky base. According to tradition, all malefactors who visit the island do not receive the favor of Buddha, and have been required to take the fatal leap from the top of this precipice to the waters below. The influence of the priest must therefore necessarily be great over the outlaws that roam the China sea.

When the worshipper visits the temple, it is necessary to leave at least a few cash as penance. If a person dies who has not been in the habit of going to the temple, it is necessary for the body to lay awhile in it before burial, or Buddha will not intercede with the evil spirit. This is often done. The temple is supplied with apartments for this purpose, and it is a rare occurrence to find them empty. Of course, Buddha receives a handsome fee for this condescension, and the old bare-headed priest is the chosen steward to take care of it.

The Chinese keep idols in their houses and shops; and the boatmen never are without them, however insignificant the craft. Adulations are daily paid to these idols, and incense burnt. The votaries appear to be devout and sincere. And yet, an impartial observer cannot but be suspicious that it is a hollow zeal, an outside devotion, and not taking a deep root in the heart. An uneducated Chinaman, with but little time or disposition for reflection, and an imperfect knowledge of his moral duties and responsibilities, cannot be deeply grounded in the faith. He is naturally superstitious, and grows to manhood in a land of superstition. He but follows in the footsteps of his ancestors while subscribing to every vagary.

At the beginning of the new year, it is customary to write some character representing a wish or virtue, on a long strip of red paper, and paste it on the wall of the house, or over the door, or on the sides of the vessel; and this is the talisman for good luck throughout the year to come. To make the charm more effective, these strips of red paper are multiplied so much, that it is common to see an entire side of the house or vessel covered with them. To give the countenance of state to this puerile rite, it is a heinous offence to tear them off, or otherwise mutilate them. They usually remain till accident or the elements have intervened for their destruction.

It is a religious ceremony to sweep the graves of one's ancestors. This observance occurs annually in the spring of the year; and whoever neglects it is the butt for the scorn of the neighborhood for many a month. This is a reasonable observance, and worthy of approval in Christian communities. The Chinaman's love for his ancestors is proverbial; and the concession of this virtue to him probably emanates from the tablets and obituary remembrances which are religiously preserved. Yet it may be, that he punctiliously observes these traditional duties more to appease the evil spirit of his ancestors, than from filial affection. It is a religious rite for the Emperor, and the chief Mandarin in every district, on the same day at the beginning of the spring to plow a furrow, and yet this probably is done to propitiate the evil spirit, not merely for a ripe and abundant harvest, but to allure the farmers by example to attend to their avocations. It also has often been said that the Emperor condescends to take hold of the plow in token of his respect for agriculture, and his constant fatherly care for the husbandman. It is likely nearer the truth to say, that he observes this custom, because it has come down to him through a long line of predecessors from the buried generations of the past. He considers it becoming to walk in their footsteps.

There is no particular day set apart for religious

observance, other than such as occurs on the annual festivals and holidays. The Chinese do not have a Sunday. They believe that the soul transmigrates at the decease of the body, into some other body or substance that has vitality. They seem to agree with Pythagoras, though they know no such person. They attach divine attributes to the Emperor, and believe him to be their representative in the great court of the celestial gods. Their religion points to the present and past. It does not seem to grasp a future world with its rewards and punishments. Their moral philosophy partakes of materialism. China has her sages, but their thoughts and philosophy point to earth, and its misery and happiness. They do not rise to the sublime idea of one and the same God ruling heaven and earth and every creature therein, from the beginning to the end for ever and ever. Much less do they appreciate the great transaction of that Being sending his only begotten Son from heaven to earth, as a sacrifice for the sins of the people. Christian missionaries have opened their eyes, and set them to thinking more or less on this subject. Christian schools have been opened at many points for the education of Chinese youth of both sexes. These schools, if they do not enlighten the heart, will enlighten their young minds with the precepts of Christianity, make them worthier people, and pave the way for a closer affinity of feeling, thought and action, between Christian and Pagan communities.

CHAPTER XXXVI.

BOTANY.— MINERALOGY.

THE bamboo abounds in China, and is profitably used in a variety of ways. It is a staple which takes the place of wood in many respects, as used in other countries. The willow is found in many parts of the empire, and is worked into baskets, and other useful articles. There are several species. One kind attains a large size. The girth is from five to ten feet. Then there is the camphor tree, from which is obtained camphor. The log is sawed into thin boards, and therewith are manufactured boxes and trunks, celebrated for preserving furs and garments from the encroachments of the moth and the mold. The tallow tree is also grown, exuding its fatty juices, and its seeds yielding vegetable oil. The fruit trees embrace the plumb, apricot, peach, fig, orange, quince pomegranate, cocoanut, pine apple, lime, hazel nut, chestnut, and walnut. There is also the paper tree, from the inner bark of which paper is manufactured extensively. The Chinese call it *Koo-soo*. They likewise have the cypress, yew, and pine. The leading shrubbery plants are the tea and the mulberry; and, as is universally known, these two plants underlie the fame and wealth of the country. The rose of innumerable variety flourishes, and the passion flower with its white, red and purple tints. The honeysuckle and the wild rose are everywhere seen in beautiful luxuriance. But all these flowers are devoid of the aroma that makes them so delightful in other lands. They are charming to the eye, but do not scent the air with delicious, rosy fragrance. Their dazzling hues bewilder the sight, but fail of other agreeable sensations.

China has its share of the mineral productions of the earth. About all that are elsewhere found, with the exception of platina, may also be found in some of the eighteen provinces. Gold and silver is found in the province of Yun-nan, and the former is also washed from the sands of the Yangtze river above Han Kow. Coals of a bituminous character and fair quality are obtainable in the same regions. The silver is of great fineness and purity, and a considerable amount leaves the kingdom every year in exchange for opium. Quicksilver is used for coloring and medicine. Vast quantities of copper are used for the making of the currency called *cash*, and it as well as brass, is worked into a variety of manufactures. They do not appear to get enough lead or tin or zinc to satisfy the home demand, as the custom house returns exhibit a large importation every year. They have gypsum, alum, and nitre. They also have porcelain earth, which has enabled them so long to monopolize the manufacture of porcelain, commonly called china ware. The supply thus far has equalled the demand, and the beds from which it is procured appear to be inexhaustible. This manufacture has been suspended of late years, in consequence of the presence of the rebels. They have overrun the country where this substance is found, and rendered it unsafe for the capitalists engaged in the manufacture, to continue the work for the present. The lime burner has no difficulty in getting stone for lime, and of the best quality. It is used extensively and constantly, no nation uses more. It is furnished in ordinary times at about one half its cost in the United States.

The most authentic accounts do not accord to China many of the precious stones. It has the jade, amber, and the agate in profusion, as well as the jasper, the amethyst and other species of quartz. But the diamond, the emerald, the beryl, must be looked for elsewhere, with any degree of success. Pearls both large and small are obtainable. Their scarcity, however, keeps them at a high price. The Chinese women are very fond of bedecking their persons with ornaments. The men wear bracelets and large finger-rings. The women in addition wear a gay head dress, if by hook or crook they can procure it. The women also have necklaces, and wear richly embroidered satin shoes and slippers, interworked with pearls. Silver ornaments of curious and various workmanship are those most sought after by all classes. Occasionally among the rich class the most precious stones are worn. It is rare however, to see the diamond, not because the wealth is lacking to pay for it, but on account of its scarcity. To make up this deficiency of supply, there are many imitations of the precious jewel. Manufactures of the spurious article meet with but little patronage, for their customers are too well posted to be often misled. The loot brought away by the British and French from the Emperor's palace, contained many priceless gems that had been gathering there during a term of time, no person knows how long. They had come there as tribute from Thibet and Tartary, and from the confines of upper India, and from remote islands in southern seas. Chinese are proverbial for their undying attachment for home; and yet they have roamed from time to time over all the Eastern oceans, and colonized many of the islands. Desirous of retaining the protecting ægis of their mother country, they have propitiated the Emperor with largesses and tribute from almost every clime. Many of the lawless rovers of those seas, it is said, have often had forgiveness of their sins, by contributions from their valuable captures. Argosies trading to Malacca and the shores of Persia, have returned heavily ladened with the priceless gems of those latitudes. From these various sources, have the Mandarins and gentry been enabled to gratify their extravagant cravings for the luxuries and riches of other countries — till the abundance in which precious stones are used, has superinduced the belief that they were indigenous to China. A great fallacy. Besides, it is found upon close scrutiny, that numerous stones of the quartz species owe their almost dazzling brilliancy to the refinement of artistical skill. In this kind of workmanship the Chinese equal, if they do not surpass, the artisans of other nations.

CHAPTER XXXVII.

THE FUTURE.

CHINA has had a long past. Amid the mutilations and revolutions of contemporaneous governments for sixty centuries, this "middle kingdom" has kept its course. True, the seat of dominion has been occupied by different dynasties, and the people of adjoining realms have crossed the border, but the manners, thoughts, and institutions of the country, have continued essentially the same. Tartary made its mark; and, by seating its imperial blood upon the throne, has drawn largely upon the royal exchequer, and wielded the sceptre. But tradition or written history fails to show a radical change in the virtues and vices, habits and opinions, of the people, or in the former policy of governmental action. From the first, it has been a despotic government, the will of the chief being the supreme law of the land. It has always claimed to be parental in cherishing the temporal interests of the inhabitants, and punishing their vices. The rulers have regarded the submission and obedience of the ruled, as the tokens of their assent to the central authority, and of their desire for its continuance. The rulers have viewed such acquiescence in the same light and of the same significance as the ballot is wont to be estimated in the revolutions of later times. From the first, also, the Emperor has assumed the heavenly character, and claimed to be the earthly vicegerent of the great and mysterious ruler of heaven. This divine attribute has been claimed so long and with such pertinacity, from age to age, that the present generation regard it as sacrilege even to question its existence. Entrenched behind the protection of this pretended influence with heaven, and their constantly asserted fatherly guardianship of the children of the earth, the emperors of all dynasties have hitherto successfully veiled the eyes of the people, and transmitted the imperial dominion from reign to reign.

Fable shrouds the early periods of Chinese history, and much of its authenticity rests upon legends and tradition. Enough light is shed to satisfy the candid enquirer, that civilization had existed and attained much progress when it was only dawning upon the nations of the western hemisphere. It is evident that the imperial dominion was shared but once. From the year of our Lord 300 to the year 600, the empire was divided into three states. After remaining in this distracted condition for about three centuries, (some traditions terminating it in the year of our Lord 585) it was again united under one ruler.

Three hundred years afterwards there was another contest for the dominion, but after fifty years of fighting, pacification ensued upon the establishment of the T'soong dynasty, and a Chinaman named Tai-soo ascended the throne. The Tartars, however, were not content; and after three or four decades of years they compelled the reigning dynasty to accept the assistance of the Mongols. The discontented Tartars were foiled in their revolutionary efforts, and a new dynasty was founded in the person of Kublai Khan. This change shocked the public mind the more, because the new Emperor removed the seat of the general government from the old and time-honored capital of Nankin, to the northern city of Pekin, where it has remained ever since. The public tranquillity continued till about the year 1350, when it was again disturbed, and resulted in the re-establishment of the Ming dynasty in the person of Hong-woo. Two centuries and a half now ensued of public prosperity, progress, and peace. The Mantchoo Tartars, about the year 1600, commenced war upon the reigning dynasty, and after convulsing the country with their hostilities for a quarter of a century, established the present imperial house, and a Mant-choo named Shun-chy, the descendant of mixed Mongol and Tartar races, ascended the imperial throne. The educated classes in China name twenty-six different dynasties, and count two hundred and thirty-six names, as the number of their sovereigns.

Upon the assumption of power by Shun-chy, a long term of peace ensued. The authority of the government was strengthened, more liberal and enlightened views upon the subjects of commerce and religion obtained, insomuch that the late Emperor Heen-fung proclaimed toleration to foreign commerce and the Christian religion. In the year 1849, there was a rising of the people in the south, near Canton. The insubordination spread, till a large army with banners had gathered in the Province. In a short time it progressed northward, subsisting upon the people as it passed along, and all the while adding to its numbers. It was under the lead of a person styled Taeping Wang. He proclaimed the object of this demonstration to be, the overthrow of the reigning dynasty, and the establishment of his person instead, as the representative of the first native Chinese dynasty. He took many large cities, and finally conquered Nankin in the following year of 1850, which he has ever since held, and where he proclaims he has established the seat of the Taeping government. His possession of this old capital of the empire, however, has not been undisturbed. The armies of the reigning dynasty have repeatedly besieged it and attempted to gain the possession, but all their efforts thus far have been in vain. On the contrary, instead of being confined to defensive operations, this new power has successfully executed many an offensive movement. It has taken the great cities of Soo-choo, Hang-chow, and Ningpo. It has overrun and subdued to its sway two thirds of the provinces of the two Kiangs with their eighty millions of people, and taken possession of innumerable villages and hamlets. In many long and bloody battles, it has shown itself an overmatch for the imperial power. Single handed it would seem to possess the resources and strength to more than cope with its adversary, and in due time gain the diadem of the reigning Emperor. Nevertheless, its future is uncertain and cloudy. The authorities of Great Britain and France appear to have resolved to aid the Emperor in crushing it. They have lent their counsels and forces for several months past. The aspect of this great and vindictive civil war has, in the meantime, materially changed; and unless the Taepings possess an unexpected recuperative energy and power, the chances are against the continuance of their sway, and in favor of the final re-ascendency of the imperial rule.

The future of China depends, in some particulars, upon the issue. A successful result to the Taepings would probably accelerate the dissemination of Christian institutions far and wide among the Chinese. An augmentation and increased facility of commercial intercourse would also probably be the consequences, if the new dynasty observed in good faith the treaty arrangements that the old dynasty has concluded with foreign nations. Whether it would be in the power of the new dynasty to act in good faith, would essentially depend upon its ability to establish and set in motion a new government in all its executive branches, and maintain order, and preserve the public peace. Its followers have been engaged so long in war, plundering from the laboring classes whatever their wants or fancy may have dictated, living, so to speak, a roving and dissolute life, makes it questionable whether their rulers in the time of peace would be able to maintain the supremacy of the laws, and afford proper protection to all persons and interests within the pale of their jurisdiction. This earnest of the future has not yet been given, by their civil administration over the country or cities and villages they have subjugated. Instead thereof, anarchy seems to be the counterpart of conquest.

Such is China and the Chinese.

The United States is nearer than either of the other treaty powers. The people of the former country do not crave dominion. They ask open ports and unfettered commerce. In sending civil and naval officers thither, the government simply desires to extend to its citizens the protection of the flag. Neutral in all that relates to the domestic troubles and internal commotions of China, the United States claims and will have all the immunities and rights which are accorded to other nations. Hitherto the government has made itself known, its laws and institutions felt, and its starry banner respected among the countries and people of both hemispheres; and God grant that, having brushed away the cloud which now lowers over the land, as will surely be the case, the great Republic of the West may continue to pursue its useful and glorious career to the end of time.

THE END.

www.ingramcontent.com/pod-product-compliance
Lightning Source LLC
Chambersburg PA
CBHW020825230426
43666CB00007B/1104